W9-BPL-742

China

Other Books of Related Interest:

Opposing Viewpoints Series

Globalization

Human Rights

Tibet

The United Nations

The World Trade Organization

Current Controversies Series

Capitalism

Fair Trade

Importing from China

The World Economy

At Issue Series

Does the World Hate the U.S.?

Is the World Experiencing an Energy Crisis?

Should the U.S. Close Its Borders?

What Is the Impact of Emigration?

"Congress shall make no law ... abridging the freedom of speech, or of the press."

First Amendment to the U.S. Constitution

The basic foundation of our democracy is the First Amendment guarantee of freedom of expression. The Opposing Viewpoints Series is dedicated to the concept of this basic freedom and the idea that it is more important to practice it than to enshrine it.

OPPOSING VIEWPOINTS® SERIES

China

Noah Berlatsky, Book Editor

GREENHAVEN PRESS
A part of Gale, Cengage Learning

GALE
CENGAGE Learning™

Detroit • New York • San Francisco • New Haven, Conn • Waterville, Maine • London

Christine Nasso, *Publisher*
Elizabeth Des Chenes, *Managing Editor*

© 2010 Greenhaven Press, a part of Gale, Cengage Learning.

Gale and Greenhaven Press are registered trademarks used herein under license.

For more information, contact:
Greenhaven Press
27500 Drake Rd.
Farmington Hills, MI 48331-3535
Or you can visit our Internet site at gale.cengage.com

For product information and technology assistance, contact us at

Gale Customer Support, 1-800-877-4253
For permission to use material from this text or product, submit all requests online at
www.cengage.com/permissions

Further permissions questions can be emailed to permissionrequest@cengage.com

Articles in Greenhaven Press anthologies are often edited for length to meet page requirements. In addition, original titles of these works are changed to clearly present the main thesis and to explicitly indicate the author's opinion. Every effort is made to ensure that Greenhaven Press accurately reflects the original intent of the authors. Every effort has been made to trace the owners of copyrighted material.

Cover photograph © Digital Vision/Getty Images.

LIBRARY OF CONGRESS CATALOGING-IN-PUBLICATION DATA

China / Noah Berlatsky, book editor.
   p. cm. -- (Opposing viewpoints)
   Includes bibliographical references and index.
   ISBN 978-0-7377-4765-2 (hardcover) -- ISBN 978-0-7377-4766-9 (pbk.)
   1. China--Politics and government--Juvenile literature. 2. Human rights--China-- Juvenile literature. 3. China--Military policy--Juvenile literature. 4. China-- Foreign relations--Juvenile literature. 5. China--Economic conditions--Juvenile literature. 6. China--Environmental conditions--Juvenile literature. 7. Environmental protection--China--Juvenile literature. I. Berlatsky, Noah.
   DS779.4.C44 2010
   951.06--dc22
                                                    2009045725

Printed in the United States of America
1 2 3 4 5 6 7 14 13 12 11 10

Contents

Why Consider Opposing Viewpoints?   11

Introduction   14

Chapter 1: What Is the Status of Human Rights and Democracy in China?

Chapter Preface   19

1. China Is Not Moving Toward Democracy   21
   Ying Ma

2. China Is Moving Toward Democracy   31
   Henry S. Rowen

3. China Must Be Convinced of the Benefits   39
   of Democracy
   Arthur Kroeber

4. China Is Committed to Human Rights   44
   Ming Wan

5. China Abuses Human Rights   54
   Amnesty International

6. Human Rights Must Be the Most Important   63
   Issue Between the United States and China
   Wei Jingsheng

Periodical Bibliography   68

Chapter 2: How Is China Handling Its Economic Challenges?

Chapter Preface   70

1. The Global Recession Did Not Weaken   72
   China's Economy
   Jeff Nielson

2. The Global Recession Weakened
   China's Economy
   Nouriel Roubini   **77**

3. Free Trade with China Benefits Both
   China and the United States
   James A. Dorn   **83**

4. Free Trade with China Benefits China
   but Hurts the United States
   James Parks   **88**

5. Trade Imbalances Are Dangerous for Both
   the United States and China
   Peter Navarro   **94**

6. China Must Do More to Combat Intellectual
   Property Piracy
   U.S. Chamber of Commerce   **99**

7. Business Must Combat Chinese Intellectual
   Property Piracy
   David Wolf   **107**

8. Chinese Intellectual Property Piracy
   Cannot Be Avoided
   Henry Blodget   **112**

Periodical Bibliography   **118**

Chapter 3: Is China's Military a Threat?

Chapter Preface   **120**

1. China's Military Buildup Is a Threat   **122**
   to U.S. Interests
   John J. Tkacik Jr.

2. China's Military Buildup Is Not a Threat   **129**
   to Legitimate U.S. Interests
   Doug Bandow

3. China Can Aid Nuclear Nonproliferation   135
   Xiaohui (Anne) Wu

4. China Is Behind the North Korean Threat   140
   Anne Applebaum

5. China Can Help Confront the   144
   North Korean Threat
   Martin Malin and Hui Zhang

6. China Remains a Threat to Taiwan   149
   J. Michael Cole

7. China-Taiwan Relations Are Improving   154
   Clifford Coonan

Periodical Bibliography   160

Chapter 4: Is China Protecting the Environment?

Chapter Preface   162

1. China's Air Pollution Is Improving   164
   Tini Tran

2. China Must Do More to Address   170
   Air Pollution
   Juli S. Kim

3. China Is Addressing Climate Change   180
   Steven Hayward

4. China Must Do More on Climate Change   185
   Bruce Stokes

Periodical Bibliography   191

For Further Discussion   192

Organizations to Contact   194

Bibliography of Books   200

Index   204

Why Consider Opposing Viewpoints?

> *"The only way in which a human being can make some approach to knowing the whole of a subject is by hearing what can be said about it by persons of every variety of opinion and studying all modes in which it can be looked at by every character of mind. No wise man ever acquired his wisdom in any mode but this."*
>
> *John Stuart Mill*

In our media-intensive culture it is not difficult to find differing opinions. Thousands of newspapers and magazines and dozens of radio and television talk shows resound with differing points of view. The difficulty lies in deciding which opinion to agree with and which "experts" seem the most credible. The more inundated we become with differing opinions and claims, the more essential it is to hone critical reading and thinking skills to evaluate these ideas. Opposing Viewpoints books address this problem directly by presenting stimulating debates that can be used to enhance and teach these skills. The varied opinions contained in each book examine many different aspects of a single issue. While examining these conveniently edited opposing views, readers can develop critical thinking skills such as the ability to compare and contrast authors' credibility, facts, argumentation styles, use of persuasive techniques, and other stylistic tools. In short, the Opposing Viewpoints Series is an ideal way to attain the higher-level thinking and reading skills so essential in a culture of diverse and contradictory opinions.

In addition to providing a tool for critical thinking, Opposing Viewpoints books challenge readers to question their own strongly held opinions and assumptions. Most people form their opinions on the basis of upbringing, peer pressure, and personal, cultural, or professional bias. By reading carefully balanced opposing views, readers must directly confront new ideas as well as the opinions of those with whom they disagree. This is not to argue simplistically that everyone who reads opposing views will—or should—change his or her opinion. Instead, the series enhances readers' understanding of their own views by encouraging confrontation with opposing ideas. Careful examination of others' views can lead to the readers' understanding of the logical inconsistencies in their own opinions, perspective on why they hold an opinion, and the consideration of the possibility that their opinion requires further evaluation.

Evaluating Other Opinions

To ensure that this type of examination occurs, Opposing Viewpoints books present all types of opinions. Prominent spokespeople on different sides of each issue as well as well-known professionals from many disciplines challenge the reader. An additional goal of the series is to provide a forum for other, less known, or even unpopular viewpoints. The opinion of an ordinary person who has had to make the decision to cut off life support from a terminally ill relative, for example, may be just as valuable and provide just as much insight as a medical ethicist's professional opinion. The editors have two additional purposes in including these less known views. One, the editors encourage readers to respect others' opinions—even when not enhanced by professional credibility. It is only by reading or listening to and objectively evaluating others' ideas that one can determine whether they are worthy of consideration. Two, the inclusion of such viewpoints encourages the important critical thinking skill of objectively evaluating an author's credentials and bias. This evaluation will illuminate an author's reasons for taking a particular stance on an issue and will aid in readers' evaluation of the author's ideas.

It is our hope that these books will give readers a deeper understanding of the issues debated and an appreciation of the complexity of even seemingly simple issues when good and honest people disagree. This awareness is particularly important in a democratic society such as ours in which people enter into public debate to determine the common good. Those with whom one disagrees should not be regarded as enemies but rather as people whose views deserve careful examination and may shed light on one's own.

Thomas Jefferson once said that "difference of opinion leads to inquiry, and inquiry to truth." Jefferson, a broadly educated man, argued that "if a nation expects to be ignorant and free . . . it expects what never was and never will be." As individuals and as a nation, it is imperative that we consider the opinions of others and examine them with skill and discernment. The Opposing Viewpoints Series is intended to help readers achieve this goal.

David L. Bender and Bruno Leone,
Founders

Introduction

"While sitting in the courtyard with my family, I heard intense gunfire. A tragedy to shock the world had not been averted, and was happening after all."

Zhao Ziyang, former Chinese Communist Party general secretary, writing about the government crackdown on the Tiananmen Square protests in his posthumous book, Prisoner of the State: The Secret Journal of Zhao Ziyang.

At the beginning of 2009, China's gross domestic product, a measure of all goods and services produced in the country, was $27 trillion yuan. Having passed Germany, China had become the third-largest economy in the world, behind only Japan and the United States. Reporter Ashley Seager noted in an article for the *Guardian* that overtaking Germany capped a remarkable period in which "the Chinese economy has grown tenfold in three decades."

The amazing growth of the Chinese economy has caused vast changes throughout China. As just one example, Leslie T. Chang, writing in a 2008 article in *National Geographic*, noted that "a decade ago most cars belonged to state enterprises; now many families own one. In 1998, when the government launched reforms to commercialize the housing market, it was the rare person who owned an apartment. Today home ownership is common."

For years, some analysts have claimed that the growth and liberalization of China's economy would result in greater political freedom for its people. However, such freedom has been very slow in coming. Despite all the economic transformation in China, the country continues to be politically undemocratic.

To understand how China has managed to open up economically but not politically, it is useful to go back to the moment in recent Chinese history when a real democratic revolution seemed most possible—the 1989 protests in Tiananmen Square.

By the late 1970s, the strict controlled economy and bloody repression favored by leader Mao Zedong had become unpopular with both Chinese leaders and people. Thus, through the 1980s, political leader Deng Xiaoping steered China away from the strict controlled economy and toward economic liberalization, including opening China's economy to more foreign trade.

However, many people in China wanted not just more economic opportunity, but a greater voice in government. As long as economic expansion went smoothly, these desires could be contained. However, in 1988–1989, economic expansion had become out of control, resulting in 30 percent inflation and factory closures as the government struggled to cool the overheating economy. At the same time, in 1989, the Soviet Union pulled back support for Communist totalitarian regimes in Eastern Europe, and as a result nations like Poland, Czechoslovakia, and Hungary experienced largely peaceful revolutions and established democratic governments. Claudia Rossett, who reported from Tiananmen Square during the protests, remembered twenty years later for *Forbes* that at the time "around the globe, the push for democracy seemed contagious." Economic anger and foreign examples of regime change were a powerful combination.

On April 15, 1989, Chinese official Hu Yaobang died. Hu, an aide to Deng, had been supportive of democratic reform and had many ties to Chinese intellectuals and democracy supporters. He had fallen from favor some years before his death, but he retained some authority and much popularity. University students in Beijing gathered in Tiananmen Square to honor Hu's memory. These rallies quickly evolved into major protests with one hundred thousand students occupying the square and "an estimated 1 million-plus students and workers" joining in with similar protests nationwide, according to Charles Recknagal writing in 2009 at *Radio Free Europe/ Radio Liberty Online*.

The protests prompted a major debate within the government leadership. Reformers such as Zhao Ziyang, the Communist Party general secretary, called for a moderate response. Others, however, were less conciliatory. Wang Zhen, who had been a general under Mao, is quoted by John Chan at the World Socialist Web site as responding to the impasse at Tiananmen Square by declaring, "Those goddamn bastards! Who do they think they are, trampling on sacred ground like Tiananmen so long?! They're really asking for it! We should send the troops right now to grab those counter-revolutionaries, Comrade Xiaoping! What's the People's Liberation Army for, anyway? What are the martial law troops for? They're not supposed to just sit around and eat! . . . We've got to do it or the common people will rebel! Anybody who tries to overthrow the Communist Party deserves death and no burial!"

Eventually, Wang's position won out. Zhao was placed under house arrest, where he remained until his death in 2005. Martial law was declared on May 20. Students staved off one effort to retake the city when the military was unwilling to use deadly force. On June 4, however, soldiers firing live ammunition retook the square. The BBC reported at the time that "several hundred civilians have been shot dead by the Chinese army during a bloody military operation." Later estimates suggested that the death toll may have been as high as a thousand or more.

Following the Tiananmen Square crackdown, pro-reformers within the government were purged and leaders of the protests were jailed. Some party officials wanted to roll back economic reforms. However, these officials lost out, just as had those who wanted to expand democratic opportunity. China continued to pursue economic reform while limiting democratic change.

Part of limiting democratic change, for the Chinese government, has been attempting to forget Tiananmen Square. It is illegal in China to debate the events of Tiananmen, and the military was out in force on June 4, 2009, the twentieth anniversary of the protests, to prevent any commemoration. Some of the Chinese people, like their government, seem ready, at least for the moment, to forget Tiananmen as well. Reporter Antoaneta Bezlova writing in the *Asia Times* quoted a philosophy student in Beijing in 2009 as stating, "In 1989 they [students] all believed in Western democracy. That is why they even had the Statue of Liberty on Tiananmen Square. . . . But I think China should follow its own path of development in politics as well as economy, and not be a copycat of the West. We have done that long enough."

Still, remembered or forgotten, the tensions that caused Tiananmen remain important in China today. This is evident in the questions posed by the chapter titles of this book: What Is the Status of Human Rights and Democracy in China? How Is China Handling Its Economic Challenges? Is China's Military a Threat? Is China Protecting the Environment? China continues to try to balance force, economic expansion, and the desires of its people for democracy and health. As the third-largest world economy—and perhaps someday as the first—the decisions it makes will affect not only China itself, but the world as a whole.

CHAPTER 1

What Is the Status of Human Rights and Democracy in China?

Chapter Preface

China's government is authoritarian and undemocratic. Leaders are for the most part appointed and not elected. Media in China are regulated, and protest against the government is strictly limited.

One of the most contentious human rights issues in China in recent years involves Falun Gong. Falun Gong is a spiritual practice that includes exercises and the study of several books. It was founded by Li Hongzhi in 1992; by 1998 China claimed that there were 70 million practitioners.

Communism has long denounced religions of many sorts, and the Communist Party in China suppressed all forms of religious observance for many years. These restrictions have been lifted in some ways recently, but mistrust of religion persists. Thus, Michael Lestz, writing in *Religion in the News* in 1999, argued that the Chinese government was leery of the Falun Gong because "it represents a large organization independent of the state that violates the unwritten 'rules of engagement' that govern the relations between the state and such organizations." The Chinese government, for its part, argues that Falun Gong is a cult that misleads its members; Chinese scientists denounced it as "anti-humanity, anti-society, and anti-science" according to a report on the official government Web site Permanent Mission of the People's Republic of China to the UN.

For whatever the reason, however, the Chinese government has for years attempted to discredit Falung Gong through the media, and has arrested and persecuted its practitioners. On February 5, 2000, for example, the BBC reported that "thousands of Falun Gong members have been arrested and several of its leaders sentenced to long prison terms as part of a crackdown on the movement by the Chinese government."

Similarly, in 2008 in the run-up to the Olympic Games the Chinese government arrested more than fifteen hundred Falun Gong practitioners.

The Chinese government has also been accused of torturing Falun Gong members following their arrests. In the worst cases, China has been accused of murdering thousands or even tens of thousands of Falun Gong prisoners, the *Epoch Times* reported in 2008, "so their organs could be sold in lucrative transplant deals." China has denied these reports— though it has admitted to harvesting organs from executed prisoners.

China continues to maintain that the Falun Gong is a legitimate threat which must be dealt with for the security of the state. Human rights organizations such as Amnesty International, on the other hand, continue to maintain that China's treatment of Falun Gong practitioners is unwarranted and inhumane. In either case, the fate of Falun Gong practitioners demonstrates what is at stake for individuals and the government in the following viewpoints about democracy, openness, and human rights in China.

> "Despite the wishes of the United States
> or the efforts of Chinese citizens, the
> Chinese government has so far quashed
> and neutralized pressure for fundamen-
> tal political change."

China Is Not Moving Toward Democracy

Ying Ma

Ying Ma is a National Research Initiative fellow at the American Enterprise Institute. In the following viewpoint, she argues that while China observers have been predicting that China's encounters with market forces or liberal institutions would spur democratic change, this has proven to be incorrect. While China has become more pluralistic and multifaceted with the introduction of Western technology and capital, the Chinese government is unwilling to relinquish its monopoly on power. While there are many Chinese citizens who are pressing for democracy, there is also widespread anti-Americanism and nationalism. These pervasive attitudes create an environment less receptive to the virtues of democratization. Perhaps one day, the author concludes, democracy will come to China—but it won't be anytime soon.

As you read, consider the following questions:

1. Why, according to the viewpoint, is the United States so invested in bringing democracy to China?

2. Give an example of the governmental repression and injustice in China, provided by the viewpoint.

3. The viewpoint suggests many ways in which the United States could help spur democratization in China—name one.

For more than a decade, successive U.S. presidents have declared that political liberalization leading ultimately to democratization in China would be desirable and decidedly in America's—and the world's—interests. The Clinton administration, after some initial tortuous twists and turns, fashioned a policy of "constructive engagement" with the Chinese government that called for close bilateral economic and political cooperation along with U.S. advocacy for democracy, open markets and human rights in China. The George W. Bush administration, though openly suspicious of China's opaque military buildup and strategic intentions, has exhorted China to become a "responsible stakeholder" of the international community while urging it to embrace democracy. To Washington, a China that is headed down a democratic path—even as it amasses military, political, and economic might—would offer the best assurance for peace, prosperity and cooperation with the United States and the world.

China, however, appears immune to and unmoved by U.S. wishes. American democracy promotion—ranging from economic engagement to democracy programs to lofty rhetoric—has not halted the speed at which the Chinese authoritarian behemoth presses on with grave human rights abuses. For now, U.S. hopes remain just hopes.

The reasons for democracy's slow boat to China are complicated: They range from American delusions to Chinese authoritarian resilience to Chinese nationalism. Far less complicated is the reality that as the United States trumpets democracy worldwide as a strategic objective and a sign of human progress, China is unabashedly providing a counterexample. Successful democratization in China, therefore, will not only usher in freedom for 1.3 billion Chinese citizens, but also strike a blow against the stubbornness of authoritarianism worldwide. It is therefore vital for U.S. policymakers to examine China's success in resisting democratization, reassess the tools and assumptions of current democracy promotion efforts, and think of new ways to remove the roadblocks to freedom.

Inevitable Democracy?

Many China observers have long been predicting that China's encounter with market forces or liberal institutions and instruments from the West would spur inevitable democratic change. These observers have been right that China would become more pluralistic and multifaceted. But they have been delusional in thinking that Chinese leaders would simply roll over and relinquish power when presented with new challenges to their rule. On everything ranging from trade to the Internet, from village elections to the rule of law, Chinese rulers have consistently proven China optimists wrong.

Certainly, the lack of political progress was not what successive Republican and Democratic administrations promised. In lobbying for continued trade with China, President Bill Clinton predicted in 2000, "We will be unleashing forces no totalitarian operation rooted in last century's industrial society can control." President George W. Bush reiterated Clinton's prediction in 2005: "I believe a whiff of freedom in the marketplace will cause there to be more demand for democracy." Just how China is to proceed from "a whiff of freedom" to democracy no one knows. Meanwhile, the CCP [Chinese Communist Party] is determined to show otherwise: It continues to gobble up Western technology, know-how, and capital without relinquishing its monopoly on power.

To Washington, all good things go together. If China encountered some element of what exists in a democratic society, many have argued, it would be unable to stop that element's accompanying democratic attributes from seeping into society as a whole. When the Chinese government institutionalized nationwide rural village elections in 1998, numerous observers believed they would inevitably pave the way for broader democratization throughout the country. When the Chinese government agreed to conduct rule-of-law cooperation with the United States on legal training, education, and administrative and commercial law in 1997 and 1998, government and academic experts predicted that any progress made in the less politically sensitive legal areas would inevitably lead to liberalization in the political rule of law. When the Internet revolution arrived in China in the late 1990s, Americans were sure that the Chinese government would quickly succumb to the democratizing powers of the free flow of information.

Each time, however, China showed that it was determined to extract the economic or governing benefits of liberalizing forces and instruments while stifling their political powers. Though millions of villagers throughout China have now experienced elections firsthand, such elections are deeply flawed. Many are uncompetitive; many others provide little or no choice over the slate of candidates; fraud is rampant; and those elected, fairly or not, often wield little decision-making power. Furthermore, the government shows little interest in expanding the elections to the national level. On the rule of law, though China now eagerly participates in rule-of-law exchanges with the United States, it has permitted legal reforms for the purpose of facilitating economic development and making its governance more efficacious, not more democratic. As such, Beijing has limited legal reform only to politically safe areas, such as commercial and administrative law, and has barred legal reform from politically sensitive areas such as political dissent, labor unrest, and religious freedom. As for the Internet, though China eagerly embraced it as a vehicle for economic modernization and technological advancement, it has aggressively neutralized the medium's democratizing effects. Though the Chinese online population exploded from a paltry 620,000 in October 1997 to about 123 million in July 2006, the Chinese government uses sophisticated technology and some 50,000 Internet police to censor Internet content; it regularly makes high-profile arrests of cyber-dissidents and has intimidated both Western and domestic companies to engage in self-censorship.

Daily Life in China

Fortunately, American delusions and Chinese authoritarianism have not stopped the Chinese people from fighting against government repression and injustice. Economic modernization may not have led to political liberalization, but it has led to a much more pluralistic society, offering many more opportunities and outlets for dissent. Unfortunately, just as Beijing has neutralized the democratizing powers of market forces or liberal instruments and institutions, it has also aggressively stifled the democratizing effect of increased social pluralism.

Today, massive unemployment and unrest plague Chinese society. Two and a half decades of economic liberalization have resulted in the state's withdrawal from the economy and social welfare network. As a result, the official registered unemployment rate in urban areas hovers at 4.2 percent. In rural areas, the unemployment rate could be as high as 20 percent. At any given moment, there are over 120 million rural migrant workers roaming the streets of Chinese cities looking for jobs. Riots take place in China every day. The Ministry of Public Security reported 10,000 protests throughout the country in 1994; 58,000 protests in 2003; 74,000 in 2004; and

87,000 in 2005. Against the backdrop of unrest and unemployment, ordinary citizens—in particular peasants—are clamoring for the central government to address their grievances on the local level on everything from corruption to poor health care. In 2004, they filed 10 million petitions for intervention from Beijing; in 2005, they filed 30 million.

The disgruntled are aided by support networks spawned by two-decades-plus of increasing social pluralism. Protestors and activists now rely on booming information resources, such as the Internet and mobile phones. Petitioners and disgruntled citizens are aided by a new thriving civil society, which once did not exist. Whereas in 1988 there were only 4,500 registered NGOs [nongovernmental organizations] in China, there were 288,936 registered in 2004 and 317,000 in 2006. Some estimate that there could be as many as 3 million unregistered NGOs in China today. Meanwhile, Jennifer Chou of Radio Free Asia reports that China's "vanguard" is finally coming to the aid of its "proletariat." Intellectuals, lawyers, and activists from the big cities have begun to help peasants challenge rigged village elections and uncompensated land confiscation. They have also begun to assist factory workers seeking health care and pensions, as well as religious believers fighting against persecution. Journalists, members of China's fourth estate, are increasingly pushing against the party line by reporting the pain, agony, and heroics of dissenting citizens, activists, and intellectuals alike.

To the Chinese leadership, economic development continues to be the first and foremost priority. To alleviate the political and social challenges from economic liberalization, Chinese President Hu Jintao has exhorted his cadres to build a "harmonious society," one which would alleviate regional economic disparities, combat corruption, placate protestors, and resist free elections. The government might be willing to tolerate incremental reforms and an increasingly pluralistic society, but such tolerance will be complemented by iron-fisted control of mobilization, organization, and coordination among disparate discontented societal segments. The increasing pluralism that appears as hopeful signs for political liberalization might ironically—and at least in the short term—relieve pressures for democratic change.

Anti-Americanism and Nationalism

Though the Chinese people may be pressing for their rights and better lives in their own ways, they have simultaneously exhibited unmistakable signs of anti-Americanism and nationalism that make them less receptive to the virtues of democratization.

In an era when the Chinese communist ideology has become defunct through the pursuit of market capitalism, China has aggressively maligned Western-style democracy as chaos-inducing and unsuitable for the country's current economic conditions. Chinese citizens, argues Beijing, have the duty to pursue Chinese greatness that would result in a strong China, a powerful China, deserving of influence and glory. Economic modernization is key, with social stability as a mandatory accessory. Through its media, textbooks, and propaganda machinery, Beijing emphasizes that democratization, political liberalization, a free press, and anti-government protests will only bring about the collapse of the current regime and hence are dangerous and destabilizing for Chinese society. When the United States criticizes China's human rights abuses or advocates democratization, it is therefore acting as an overbearing and domineering hegemon and is only seeking to undermine China's rise.

Ideological indoctrination has its consequences. Numerous Chinese citizens, particularly those in the emerging middle class, agree with their government that China is not ready for democratization. They see post-Soviet Russia's social instability, weakened economic growth, declining national power and overall chaos as most unappealing for China. In addition, they are deeply skeptical of U.S. motives. According to an opinion poll conducted by the Chinese newspaper *Global Times* (*Huan Qiu Shi Bao*) in 2006, some 59 percent of the Chinese people who live in urban metropolises believe that the United States is seeking to contain China, with 56.3 percent seeing the United States as China's competitor. In addition, Chinese citizens recoil at U.S. criticisms of their government's human rights abuses. A similar *Global Times* survey in 2005 reports that almost 79 percent of the respondents have negative views toward U.S. criticism of China's human rights abuses: 49.3 percent believe that the United States is attempting to destroy stability in China; 10.4 percent believe that the United States is trying to make China look bad, and 19.1 percent believe that America simply does not understand China's internal situation.

In response to the Chinese government distortions, the United States has done little to understand or assuage Chinese citizens' concerns. Most American leaders merely ignore Chinese concerns about U.S. intentions or about democratization's side effects, opting instead to reiterate the virtues of democracy in abstract terms. As President Bush emphasizes that "every human heart desires to be free," many Chinese citizens, sadly, seem to answer, "Don't be so sure."

The Future of China

Despite the wishes of the United States or the efforts of Chinese citizens, the Chinese government has so far quashed and neutralized pressure for fundamental political change. Beijing controls and stunts precisely those instruments that contribute to the success of a broad-based domestic opposition: It cracks down on political opponents, co-opts potential ones, and indoctrinates the masses. It is eagerly attempting to maximize economic modernization while minimizing its liberalizing effects. As the West awaits the next set of pressures or instruments that might force Beijing to reform internally or relinquish its authoritarian rule, the Chinese regime stands determined to remain in power.

The resilience of Chinese authoritarianism does not eliminate all possibility that U.S. economic engagement could lead to Chinese political liberalization and democratization in the long run. Resilience, however, makes that outcome much less certain or straightforward and renders America's disposition to simply wait for democracy to emerge in China increasingly unwise and untenable. The United States must do more to spur democratization in China.

At the moment, the U.S. government broadly promotes democracy in China by supporting democratic voices and institutions from within while criticizing and shaming the Chinese regime from the outside. On the former, the U.S. government provides support for a host of activities and projects that include funding for rule-of-law collaboration and village elections, direct financial aid for civil society organizations and Chinese political dissidents, broadcasting of Voice of America and Radio Free Asia Chinese-language programs, and cultural and educational exchanges. To pressure the Chinese government from the outside, the U.S. government frequently criticizes China's human rights record, presses for the release of political and religious dissidents, and publicly and privately calls for the Chinese government to undertake fundamental political reforms.

While current U.S. efforts to promote democracy in China are necessary and important, they do not always counter the sources of Chinese authoritarian resilience discussed here. Certainly, American actions will not and cannot eliminate all of these sources. For instance, the United States should not wade into the quandary of slowing Chinese economic growth and cannot stop the Chinese government from institutionalizing itself or co-opting its rival political groups. Nevertheless, Washington should and can do more to combat other sources of authoritarian resilience by strengthening China's political opposition and countering the regime's restriction of coordination goods that range from press freedoms to the ability to organize. In addition, the United States should begin a serious effort to confront the Chinese government's aggressive ideological indoctrination of its citizens against democratization.

International peace and security in the twenty-first century will depend in no small part on the future of China and its relations with the world. Peaceful democratization in China will not serve as a guarantee for peace, but it will offer much, much better prospects. Given the tremendous stakes involved, the United States should reconsider the many misplaced assumptions underpinning its China policy. It should recognize the tenacity and resilience of Chinese authoritarianism and relinquish the hope that such authoritarianism will simply and inevitably wilt in the face of U.S. wishes. It should better understand how such authoritarianism adapts to, co-opts, and compartmentalizes market forces and their various accompanying liberal attributes and find better solutions for countering it.

Perhaps one day, freedom for 1.3 billion Chinese citizens will arrive, but until then promoting liberation from the chains of Chinese communist authoritarianism will remain a slog. The United States should start slogging much more seriously today.

> *"Should China's economy and the educational attainments of its population continue to grow ... China will by 2025 be ... classed as belonging to the Free nations of the earth."*

China Is Moving Toward Democracy

Henry S. Rowen

Henry S. Rowen is director emeritus of the Asia-Pacific Research Center at the Freeman Spogli Institute for International Studies. In the following viewpoint, he argues that China's economic growth, if sustained, will lead to democratization by 2025. Rowen claims that expanding education and open markets are not compatible with autocratic rule and that China will therefore be forced to grant its people more rights.

As you read, consider the following questions:

1. According to Rowen, by 2025 China should have a gross domestic product [GDP] per capita roughly equivalent to that of what nation today?

Henry S. Rowen, "When Will the Chinese People Be Free?" *Journal of Democracy*, vol. 18, July 2007, pp. 38–42. Copyright © 2007 by National Endowment for Democracy and The Johns Hopkins University Press. Reproduced by permission.

2. In 2000, China's entire over-twenty-five population had an average of how many years of schooling?

3. In 2005, what percentage of Chinese respondents agreed with the proposition that the best economic system is "the free-market economy"?

L ittle more than a decade ago, my answer to the question [when will the Chinese people be free?] ... was the year 2015. My assessment, published in the Fall 1996 issue of *The National Interest*, began by observing that all countries (leaving aside states that make nearly all their money from oil exports) which had attained a Gross Domestic Product per capita (GDPpc)[1] of at least US$8,000 per year ... stood no worse than Partly Free in the ratings of political rights and civil liberties published annually by Freedom House (FH).

As China's economy was growing at a rate that promised to carry it to a level near or beyond that GDPpc benchmark by 2015, I reasoned that this, the world's largest country, was a good bet to move into the Partly Free category as well. Since then, China has remained deep in Not Free territory even though its civil-liberties score has improved a bit—from an absolutely abysmal 7 to a still-sorry 6 on the 7-point FH scale—while its political-rights score has remained stuck at the worst level.

Yet today [in 2007], as I survey matters from a point slightly more than mid-way between 1996 and 2015, I stand by my main conclusion: China will in the short term continue to warrant a Not Free classification, but by 2015 it should edge into the Partly Free category. Indeed, I will go further and predict that, should China's economy and the educational attainments of its population continue to grow as they have in recent years, the more than one-sixth of the world's people

1. Gross Domestic Product per capita is the total goods and services produced by a country divided by the total population.

who live in China will by 2025 be citizens of a country correctly classed as belonging to the Free nations of the earth. . . .

Growth Leads to Liberty

China's per-capita growth over the last decade has averaged a highly impressive 8.5 percent annually (reaching a GDPpc of $6,000. . .). Serious challenges lie ahead, yet given China's competent economic-policy makers, a supportable projection is an average per-capita growth rate of 7 percent a year, enough to raise GDPpc to $10,000 . . . by 2015. After that, slower workforce expansion (a product of changing demographics) plus China's expected approach toward convergence with the world's leading developed economies suggest that the growth rate will climb less steeply. Annual growth of 5 percent in GDPpc starting in 2015 will bring China to roughly $14,000 . . . by 2025, or about where Argentina is today.

Short-term disruptions would do little to disturb this projection. There was such a hitch after the Tiananmen Square massacre in 1989[2] but the growth rate subsequently recovered so robustly that the slow period was soon offset with no lasting economic effects. The prospect for sustained growth over at least the next decade appears strong.

The next question to be explored is the relation between economic development and democratic freedom. There are three possibilities: 1) Development might lead to democracy; 2) democracy might foster development; or 3) there might be a common cause driving both.

My 1996 projection was based on the first direction. This is the hypothesis, associated with [political sociologist] Seymour Martin Lipset, that only a society with educated, wealthy people can resist the appeal of demagogues. Stable democracy presupposes a certain level of accumulated human, social, and

2. Chinese government forces suppressed and killed many pro-democracy demonstrators during protests in Beijing's Tiananmen Square in 1989.

Henry S. Rowan's Predictions for China's Future			
Year	Per capita GDP	Average years of schooling	Predicted electoral rights	Predicted freedom house rating
2010	$8,500	6.3	22	Not free
2015	$10,000	6.7	43	Partly free
2020	$11,800	7.2	61	Partly free
2025	$14,000	7.7	76	Free

TAKEN FROM: Henry S. Rowan, "When Will the Chinese People Be Free?" *Journal of Democracy* 18:3, July 2007, pp. 36–52.

physical capital. A related view is that institutions which promote limited government (particularly via constraints placed on executive power) support growth.

Education promotes growth, and might also independently promote political pluralization by reducing the costs of political action in support of relatively democratic regimes. Schooling makes democratic revolutions against dictatorships more probable and successful antidemocratic coups less probable. After analyzing more than a hundred countries, [Harvard economist] Robert J. Barro found that higher incomes and higher levels of (primary) education predict higher freedoms. He also found significant time lags between the appearance of a factor positive for electoral rights and its expression in politics. He interpreted such lags as tokens of inertia in institutions affected by changes in economic and social variables, and noted that after about two decades "the level of democracy is nearly fully determined by the economic and social variables." This observation helps one to understand why a rapidly growing country such as China has a freedom rating today well below the level that its current income would predict. . . .

Other Possibilities

The second possibility is realized if the rules of electoral democracy turn out to be better on average for development than are those of dictatorships. Democracies tend to foster governmental transparency and the production of public goods while placing some limits on what rulers can steal. Yet a democracy with a populist bent can insist on economically damaging schemes for redistributing income and wealth. Barro and [New York University economist Adam] Prezworski are among those who find that democracy does not lead directly to higher growth. According to [Swedish economist] Torsten Persson and [Italian economist] Guido Tabellini, the evidence that democratizations yield economic growth is weak. They also write that "democracy" is too blunt a concept and that institutional details matter greatly. The theoretical picture remains unclear and the literature is divided.

The third possibility, that democracy and development have a common cause, finds support from [MIT economist] Daron Acemoglu and his coauthors, who argue that "though income and democracy are positively correlated, there is no evidence of a causal effect. Instead . . . historical factors appear to have shaped the divergent political and economic development paths of various societies, leading to the positive association between democracy and economic performance." These scholars see political and economic development paths as interwoven. Some countries embarked on development paths associated with democracy and economic growth, while others followed paths based on dictatorship, repression, and more limited growth.

Might there be a regional, specifically Sinitic [Chinese], effect involving the politics influenced by Chinese civilization? These also include Japan, the two Koreas, Vietnam, Singapore, and Taiwan. Today they present a mixed picture. Japan, South Korea, and Taiwan are rated Free; Singapore is Partly Free; and North Korea, Vietnam, and China are Not Free. Nonetheless, the paths carved out by Japan, South Korea, and Taiwan show that Western-style democracy can take root in Sinitic societies.

Education is crucial, and here China does not impress. In 2000, the country's entire over-25 population had only an average of 5.74 years of schooling (between all developing countries at 4.89 years and the East Asia and Pacific country average of 6.50 years). Yet large educational-improvement efforts are underway, especially in rural areas and the rapidly expanding postsecondary sector. My projection is that by 2025 the average Chinese person over 25 will have had almost eight years of formal schooling.

Between 1999 and 2005, postsecondary admissions tripled, reaching five million during the latter year. Currently China has about twenty million people with higher degrees; by 2020 there will be more than a hundred million. Although there are problems of educational quality and jobs, China's rising educational indicators bode well for both economic development and democracy.

Democracy Will Win Out

What conclusion should we draw from the scholarship so far on democracy and development? I think it is that growth-friendly policies, if consistently pursued (historically determined institutions may prevent this), lead to the accumulation of human and physical capital and the rise of limited government. Autocratic regimes in economically growing countries can delay but not ultimately stop this from happening.

China's so-far slight improvement in the FH rankings has been in the Civil Liberties category, where it has gone from a 7 (the absolute worst score) to a 6. Looking behind the FH numbers, we can identify several factors that have led to a substantial growth in personal liberties and promise more freedom to come.

The first is that a modern economy is simply not compatible with the Leninist [i.e., the style of communism developed by Russian leader Vladimir Lenin] requirement of comprehensive party and state control over society. The Chinese Communist Party (CCP) has faced a hard choice: Maintain control and risk economic stagnation and political disaffection, or let go and risk eventually losing dominance. The CCP has chosen to pull back in several domains. Most notably, it allows markets to function. It also has accorded certain legal institutions and media outlets a degree of autonomy. The CCP has become Marxist-Leninist in name only. In reality, it seeks to rule a system that might be called party-state capitalism, setting broad rules while leaving much authority to local Party figures and various private actors. Central authorities can intervene, but they ration their energies.

One might think that a party which promotes markets, has formally enrolled "capitalists," and has allowed the state sector's share of the economy to shrink has lost any plausible claim to be called communist or socialist. Phrases such as "capitalism with Chinese characteristics" and "democratic socialism" do not disguise the reality of the CCP's massive but mostly unacknowledged ideological shift. Not that there is much nostalgia for socialism—or even a Confucian [after ancient Chinese philosopher Confucius] contempt for profit: In a 2005 survey of twenty countries, China featured the highest share of respondents (74 percent) who agreed with the proposition that the best economic system is "the free-market economy."

The regime's legitimacy seems to rest on three main pillars: 1) It has brought social order after a century and a half of upheavals; 2) people's incomes are growing rapidly (even if the growth is unevenly distributed); and 3) Chinese enjoy a sense that the Beijing government is restoring China to its rightful place of prominence in the world.

Surveys show that confidence in the government is high, and people seem satisfied with the way that "democracy" is unfolding. Yet sources of discontent such as corruption, environmental damage, and sharp income inequality remain. In a departure from Chinese tradition, there is a developing attitude that individuals have rights.

Local elections, along with the aforementioned rise of certain relatively autonomous legal and media institutions, are helping to expand personal liberties and may have the potential to transform Chinese society.

> "[China] will embrace democracy only when it is convinced of democracy's superior ability to guarantee . . . political stability, improved social services and a clean government."

China Must Be Convinced of the Benefits of Democracy

Arthur Kroeber

Arthur Kroeber is the managing director of the economics research firm Dragonomics, and the publisher of the China Economic Quarterly. *In the following viewpoint, he argues that the Chinese government has taken care to address inequality, corruption, and other social and governmental problems without making a transition to democracy. Kroeber contends that the government's efforts have provided prosperity for a rising middle class, which, though relatively small, is key to maintaining the regime's power. Kroeber argues that this middle class must be convinced of the virtues of democracy if China is to end its authoritarian system of government.*

As you read, consider the following questions:

1. Uniquely among communist nations, what did China achieve in 2002, according to Kroeber?

2. China's ruling party carefully studied the collapse of what nation, according to the author?

3. According to Kroeber, the middle class of China comprises what percentage of the total Chinese population?

China is ready for democracy. The arguments against it—heard frequently not just from government officials but from members of the nation's rising "middle class"—are specious. They are motivated partly by an understandable fear of instability but more by the self-interest of the elites who now hold power.

Yet there is also little evidence that the growing dynamism of China's economy is creating space for the emergence of democratic institutions. Even as it reformed the economy, the Chinese Communist party skilfully strengthened its control over important economic actors—including virtually all of the nation's big companies. It also ensured that responses to the country's major social ills flow mainly through government channels.

Democracy Is Not Inevitable

There is a tendency among westerners who have forgotten their own history to view democracy dogmatically as an end in itself. In reality, democracy emerged principally as the best means to achieve other desirable social ends such as stable power succession, fair distribution of public goods, the resolution of conflicts between interest groups and government accountability for the use of tax money.

The party's strategy is to accomplish as many of these ends as possible within the existing political framework, thereby undercutting the argument for democratisation and power-sharing. Uniquely among communist nations, China achieved a peaceful transfer of power from one living leader to another leader who was not a family member, when Hu Jintao took over as state president from Jiang Zemin in 2002. It has laid the groundwork for another smooth transition in 2012, when vice-president Xi Jinping is expected to take over from Mr Hu.

Mr Hu and Wen Jiabao, his premier, attacked the problems of rising inequality and deteriorating social services with their "Harmonious Society" programme. This first raised farm incomes and now focuses on improving access to education and healthcare. Spending on social services rose by 28 per cent in 2007, well above the 23 per cent growth in total government expenditure and the 17 per cent rise in declared defence spending. Further big rises in social service spending are likely in the coming years.

The party has also tried to stem the tide of corruption and local government malfeasance by a host of measures which include regular rotation and term limits for officials, mandatory retirement ages and stepped-up discipline inspections. Training programmes and performance review systems have significantly raised the professionalism of officials and forced them to focus on goals such as environmental protection and responsiveness to citizen complaints, alongside the traditional economic growth targets.

None of this is accidental. As China scholar David Shambaugh details in a new book, *China's Communist Party Atrophy and Adaptation*, the party carefully studied the collapse of the Soviet Union and concluded that to avoid the same fate it needed to run a dynamic economy, restrain corruption and ensure that government stayed responsive to changing social needs. The successful execution of this strategy has resulted in what another sinologist [one who studies China], Andrew Nathan, has aptly dubbed "Resilient Authoritarianism": an autocratic system responsive enough to societal demands to keep itself in power for a long time.

Chinese Middle Class

The past decade has seen the rise of . . . a Chinese middle class, now estimated to number between 100 million and 150 million people. Though definitions vary—household income of at least $10,000 a year is one standard— middle-class families tend to own an apartment and a car, to eat out and take vacations. . . . They owe their well-being to the government's economic policies, but in private they can be very critical of the society they live in.

The state's retreat from private life has left people free to choose where to live, work, and travel, and mate- rial opportunities expand year by year. A decade ago most cars belonged to state enterprises; now many fami- lies own one. In 1998, when the government launched reforms to commercialize the housing market, it was the rare person who owned an apartment. Today home own- ership is common, and prices have risen beyond what many young couples can afford. . . .

But pick up a Chinese newspaper, and what comes through is a sense of unease at the pace of social change. Over several months in 2006, these were some of the trends covered in the *Xinmin Evening News*, a popular Shanghai daily: High school girls were suffering from eating disorders. Parents were struggling to choose a suit- able English name for their child. Teenage boys were reading novels with homosexual themes. Job seekers were besieging Buddhist temples because the word for "reclin- ing Buddha," *wofo*, sounds like the English word "offer." Unwed college students were living together.

Leslie T. Chang, National Geographic, *May 2008.*

Convincing the Middle Class

For democracy advocates inside and outside of China, the Communist party's relative success in improving its governance capacity means that arguments resting on the a priori [given] assumption of democracy's superiority will fall on deaf ears. This is particularly true because the Communists' programme especially benefits the natural constituency of a more open society. This is the so-called Chinese "middle class"—people in cities who have significant discretionary income left over after basic necessities are paid for.

Calling this group a "middle class" is severely misleading. Although large in absolute terms (perhaps 150m–200m) it is in reality a privileged elite, comprising no more than 15 per cent of the total Chinese population. Members of this class grumble about corruption but on the whole they have fared quite well from China's economic boom of the past decade. They know that if democracy were introduced tomorrow they would be outvoted and they have little interest in changing the system.

This crucial elite constituency will embrace democracy only when it is convinced of democracy's superior ability to guarantee (in the medium to long term) political stability, improved social services and a clean government accountable for its use of public funds and responsive to new social demands. This argument can be made, and it should be made. The task for democracy advocates is therefore not to lecture the Chinese on the inherent superiority of democracy, but to prove it by marshalling the evidence that it promotes stability and better satisfies social needs.

| *"China is currently adopting human rights law and is joining in the adoption of international human rights instruments law."*

China Is Committed to Human Rights

Ming Wan

Ming Wan is professor of government and politics and director of the Global Affairs Program at George Mason University. In the following viewpoint, Wan details how China has moved toward human rights law, internationally and domestically, since the late 1970s. Wan outlines the adoption of human rights law and its impact on daily life in China. While Wan acknowledges that passing human rights legislation does not always mean implementation, he argues that human rights legislation still makes a difference in China.

As you read, consider the following questions:

1. According to the viewpoint, what is one reason why China's adoption of human rights law matters?

2. How many Chinese laws have explicit human rights applications, according to the viewpoint?

Ming Wan, "Human Rights Lawmaking in China: Domestic Politics, International Law, and International Politics," *Human Rights Quarterly*, vol. 29, August 2007, pp. 727–753. Copyright © by the Johns Hopkins University Press. Reproduced by permission.

3. How are the Chinese reducing their use of the death penalty, according to the viewpoint?

China has moved toward human rights law internationally and domestically since the late 1970s. Their economic reform necessitates the introduction of law in conjunction with building a market economy. As a Permanent Member of the United Nations Security Council, China cannot avoid integrating international human rights law into its system of governance, and Beijing has found soft rights law manageable. Western rights pressure since 1989 has had an indirect impact. Beijing sees legal reform and the signing of international rights conventions as evidence of progress. While somewhat limited, China's adoption of rights laws affects how domestic politics is played out and leads to the creation of a legal profession interested in promotion of the rule of law.

China Is Adopting Human Rights Laws

China is currently adopting human rights law and is joining in the adoption of international human rights instruments law. Of the thirteen core international human rights treaties highlighted by the Office of the United Nations High Commissioner for Human Rights (OHCHR), China is now a part to six and a signatory to two. By comparison, the United States is a party to five and signatory to three and Japan is a party to eight. Both Japan and the US have signed or ratified the same eight treaties as China. Further, Chinese domestic law has expanded drastically. The National People's Congress (NPC) and its Standing Committee (NPCSC) have made more than 450 laws and legal decisions over the past two decades. In a formalistic sense, the expansion of a Chinese legal system centered on the Constitution indicates progress in rule of law relating to human rights. Additionally, numerous Chinese laws have explicit human rights applications.

The extensive human rights lawmaking in China raises two sets of questions. First, why is China interested in accepting human rights law that is bound to restrain its non-democratic party rule? Is this simply a cynical exercise of legal formalism designed to fool the international community and domestic audience? Since China is joining international human rights law and formulating domestic human rights law at the same time, it is natural to ask whether the two developments are related. Does Western pressure and Chinese response explain China's turn to human rights law? Are international human rights legal standards affecting China's domestic legal standards through a process of socialization?

Has human rights law improved Chinese citizens' rights and made democracy more likely? How has legalization affected China's domestic politics? Legal formalism does not necessarily improve human rights and it is often dismissed for precisely that reason. When it comes to human rights, Chinese legal reform is severely limited in the absence of genuine political reform to allow opposition parties to form and run for offices in free, competitive elections. Nevertheless, China's adoption of human rights law matters. With China in international human rights law, bad behavior becomes non-compliance, which entails some diplomatic costs for the government. Also, legal reform affects how domestic politics is played, with human rights implications. Law both enlarges and restricts political power. Moreover, formal legalization may lead to real improvement in the future. In fact, a focus on upstream deliberations rather than downstream behavior sheds light on what to expect in the future. Far-reaching debates over jurisprudence are taking place in China, which is already making a difference in people's lives, as reflected in increased legal cases for citizens' rights, and this may have an even more profound impact in the future.

China's Turn to Human Rights Law

China has joined numerous international human rights treaties since 1980. The OHCHR has listed forty-three international human rights treaties and protocols in its website, as of December 2006. Of the forty-three treaties and protocols, twenty-three have been approved by the United Nations General Assembly, one by the UN Economic and Social Council, two by the UN Education, Science and Culture Organization, ten by the International Labor Organization (ILO), three by the Slavery Convention, and four by the Geneva Convention.

China has become a party to eighteen human rights instruments, ratifying all but two after 1980. Additionally, China has signed two instruments. Of the twenty-three by the UN General Assembly, the OHCHR considers thirteen to be core legal instruments, of which China has joined six (CEDAW, ICERD, CAT, CRC, ICESCR, and OP-CRC-SC) and China has signed, but not ratified another two (ICCPR and OP-CRC-AC).

China is experiencing a boom in domestic lawmaking. The National People's Congress (NPC) has adopted more than 450 laws and legal decisions over the past twenty years. Wu Bangguo, the chairman of the NPC, cited more than 400 laws and legal decisions by mid 2003. The Ninth NPC and National People's Congress Standing Committee (NPCSC) (1998–2003) alone reviewed and passed seventy-four laws, eight legal interpretations, and twenty-eight legal decisions. The current NPC passed ten bills in 2003, twenty-two in 2004, and eighteen in 2005. Besides national laws (*falü*), by September 2002 the State Council had issued over 800 legally binding administrative regulations (*xingzheng fagui*) and the local governments had adopted over 8,000 local regulations (*difangxing fagui*). According to the Chinese government's plan, a Chinese legal system is taking shape and will be completed by 2010.

The fact that China is turning to law has obvious human rights implications. A shift away from rule of man necessarily improves the human rights situation. Moreover, some new Chinese laws have direct human rights applications.

Any discussion of Chinese human rights law should start with the 1982 Constitution. As the fourth constitution for the People's Republic of China (PRC), the 1982 Constitution saw marked improvements in legalizing human rights. The previous three constitutions (1954, 1975, and 1978) put human rights in Chapter Three following Chapter Two that talks about state institutions. By contrast, the 1982 Constitution lists citizens' rights in Chapter Two, which is the general practice of constitutions in the world. The 1982 Constitution has more articles (nineteen) about rights than the previous ones. This version of the Constitution was revised in 1988, 1993, 1999, and 2004. The 1999 revision added a section related to human rights in Article Five, which reads: "The People's Republic of China practices ruling the country in accordance with the law and building a socialist country of law." The March 2004 revision added a line in Article 33, which reads: "the state respects and protects human rights." The previous constitutions had no laws to substantiate the constitutional rights. By contrast, an expanding body of laws supports the 1982 Constitution. At least thirty Chinese laws have explicit human rights applications.

Limitations of Chinese Human Rights Law

It would be naïve to believe that once a country signs an international human rights treaty, its government will comply. A quick survey of the countries that have signed some of the international human rights treaties raises immediate questions about compliance. Examples include North Korea's accession to the International Covenant on Economic, Social and Cultural Rights and the International Covenant on Civil and Political Rights on 14 December 1981 and Saudi Arabia's ratification of the Convention on the Elimination of All Forms of Discrimination against Women on 7 October 2000.

It would also be naïve to think that China's human rights situation would improve once the Chinese government put

Human Rights Action Plan

China released its first human rights action plan [on April 13, 2009]. . . .

The two-year plan promises the communist government will do more to prevent illegal detention and torture, and to boost the overall living standard of minorities, women, the unemployed and the disabled.

But it says a central tenet of its policy remains ensuring Chinese people have the right to make money.

Seattle Times, April 13, 2009.

new laws on the books. To begin with, while China has made progress in legal reform, it remains a non-democratic country in which the Communist Party dominates in all aspects of political life and policy takes precedence over law. There is no question that the party wants to control the Chinese legal system as well. The party unapologetically sees its objective of "governing the country according to law" (*yifazhiguo*) as ensuring the party leadership in an institutional and legal fashion. Senior judicial officials serve the interests of the party before anything else. In fact, law has been seen and used as a new and more appropriate tool to repress dissent. Also, government officials routinely interfere in court rulings. The Chinese laws often have flaws or are not faithfully implemented. In fact, one hears complaints in China that the government should focus on implementing existing laws rather than on creating new ones. In particular, government agencies and local governments often issue regulations in different versions to ensure compliance, which is a waste of legal resources. Chinese judges, particularly on the local level, are generally low in legal training and experience. To make things worse, lawyers are routinely abused or arrested for serving as defendants against government prosecutors. Over 500 lawyers had been arrested for defending their clients in criminal cases by the end of 2002. In a high profile case, human rights lawyer Gao Zhisheng was put on a one-day trial on the charge of subversion on 12 December 2006. The trial occurred during a government crackdown on lawyers representing people suing the government.

Human Rights Legislation Still Makes a Difference in China

Despite the severe limitations discussed previously, legalization in China has important consequences for Chinese domestic politics and human rights. First, law, understood broadly, provides structures and schemes for people to carry on their daily activities within a society and between nations. As a direct result of China's legalization, Chinese citizens have gained much ground vis-à-vis the state since 1978. They live better and freer than before.

First, legalization, whether superficial or not, affects the nature of politics and power plays in China. Laws frame how politics operates in China, making some previous abusive practices—such as political campaigns—less legitimate and harder to carry out. Legal reform that began in 1978 has over time created a "serious, multi-stage, multi-arena lawmaking process" in China, away from a unified, top-down policy making system. The NPC has become an important arena for politics. Legalization also affects the relationship between state and society. A more modern and complex society requires more and better laws. As a result, Chinese jurisprudence is venturing into previously forbidden areas.

Second, legalization gives Chinese legal professionals an increasing role to play in Chinese politics. The Chinese legal profession has expanded dramatically over the past two decades. Starting from almost non-existence in the late 1970s,

China came to have over 9,500 law offices and 110,000 lawyers by 2000. Chinese lawyers have seized the opportunity to become more involved in lawmaking and regulations of state-society relations on a daily basis. Lawmaking is a complex process, which requires legal expertise. As a result, Chinese jurists, including law professors in universities and research institutions, play a prominent role in the drafting of new laws. Legal experts are also beginning to take important positions within the Chinese power hierarchy.

Third, legal reform has improved China's human rights situation even in sensitive areas. New laws put greater restrictions on state agencies. The Chinese government is now reducing its use of the death penalty—the Chinese Supreme Court must now approve all executions based on new death penalty rules enacted in October 2006—and removing the power of police to send people to education-through-labor camps without trials, both of which are major sources of human rights violations in China. Difficult as it may be, with laws on the books, Chinese lawyers and citizens have become more accustomed to using laws to defend their rights against government agencies. The Chinese courts ruled over almost 500,000 administrative justice cases in a five-year span by early 2003. The number of such cases increased from 27,125 in 1992 to 100,921 in 2001. The loss ratio for plaintiffs decreased from 35.9 percent to 28.6 percent. The loss ratio for defendants increased from 22.0 percent to 25.7 percent.

Human Rights Are Improving in China

Human rights lawmaking in China is a complex process shaped by the politics of reform and party legitimization on the domestic level and the limited enforceability of international human rights law, international legal norms, and interstate strategic interaction on the international level. Chinese domestic politics is the principal driver of China's turn to human rights law. Due to the desperate state of Chinese economy and his own vision of where China should go, Deng [Xiaoping] chose a market-oriented development strategy of economic reform and opening, a pivotal decision that led to a chain of events with intended and unintended consequences for the country. Since Deng's reform aimed at establishing economy market and integration with the global market, legal reform became necessary. While the Chinese legal reforms have been biased in favor of trade and commercial laws, this inevitably spilled over into civil and political rights, which ultimately cannot be separated from economic and social rights. The elite interests in social order and self-preservation based on the negative experience during the Cultural Revolution helped to adopt human rights norms. With communism discredited, the Chinese party-state increasingly has turned to law, while simultaneously promoting economic development and nationalism as a basis for the legitimacy of its continuous rule, and as a useful instrument for effective governance.

International factors also matter greatly in China's legal development. The success of capitalist economies, particularly in China's neighborhood, narrowed options for Chinese reformers and pointed a way out. The Chinese government also found it urgent to formulate laws more so because of China's need to integrate with the global market than because of its need to establish a domestic market. In a more direct sense, international human rights law, which had expanded since the end of the Second World War, presented a challenge for the Chinese government entering the international system in the late 1970s: to join or not to join. Beijing had little choice but to join international human rights law given its concern for its status as a major player in the United Nations system whose legitimacy it did not challenge. International human rights law, consistent with domestic laws of most advanced democracies, sets standards and frames of reference for Chinese legal debates, whether they are openly acknowledged it or not.

Western legal exchange programs for China have directly fed into the process of Chinese legal reform.

Western human rights pressure on China since the 1989 Tiananmen Incident has an indirect impact on China's human rights legalization. Beijing sees legal reform and the signing of international human rights conventions as a way to meet the West half way. The government is determinated not to have genuine political reform and not to give Chinese citizens genuine civil and political rights. This policy is the result of a belief that such actions would spell the end of the party rule and its strong interest in engaging with the West to further China's economic growth, which is also considered essential for maintaining the party rule.

The Chinese government remains in the center of the Chinese process of turning to law. Its success in economic reform and in minimizing Western political pressure in its strategic interaction with the West gives it confidence in continuing rather than reversing its current approach. As the party continues to resist a genuine political reform, it tightly controls the pace of the Chinese legal reform. At the same time, China's reform and opening over the past two decades have unleashed economic and social forces that have come into play in Chinese politics. Chinese citizens want to live better and freer.

Human rights lawmaking in a non-democracy is bound to be severely limited, which is indeed the case in China. But adoption of human rights law still matters. Legalization affects how politics operates in China. While it enhances the effectiveness of the party state in some areas, it also constrains its power in other areas. Law ultimately structures the state and state-society relationship. Legal reform has slowly but surely led to a pluralization of Chinese decision making and greater freedom for society. Legal reform also leads to the creation and expansion of a legal profession that is increasingly familiar with foreign and international laws and promotes internationalization of Chinese law.

| "The Olympic Games in Beijing brought heightened repression throughout the country as authorities tightened control over human rights defenders, religious practitioners, lawyers and journalists."

China Abuses Human Rights

Amnesty International

Amnesty International (AI) is an international nongovernmental human rights organization. In the following viewpoint, AI argues that China systematically abuses human rights by harassing human rights activists, utilizing arbitrary arrests and detention, limiting freedom of expression and freedom of religion, and harassing and repressing ethnic minorities in Tibet and the Xinjiang Uighur Autonomous Region. AI contends that human rights abuses were in many cases exacerbated by China's efforts to prepare for the Olympic Games held in Beijing in 2008.

As you read, consider the following questions:

1. According to AI, the detention of Huang Qi appeared to be connected to his work doing what?

2. According to the author, how many executions took place in China in 2008?

China—Amnesty International Report 2009, New York: Amnesty International, 2009.

3. Why has it been hard to determine the exact numbers of Tibetans detained in protests who remained in Chinese custody, in AI's opinion?

The Olympic Games in Beijing [in 2008] brought heightened repression throughout the country as authorities tightened control over human rights defenders, religious practitioners, ethnic minorities, lawyers and journalists. Following protests and unrest which began in March in Lhasa [Tibet] the government originally detained over 1,000 people. Hundreds remained in detention or were unaccounted for at year's end. The authorities used a series of violent incidents alleged to be linked to terrorists to launch a sweeping crackdown on the Uighur population in the Xinjiang Uighur Autonomous Region (XUAR).[1] Torture and other ill-treatment remained widespread. The authorities maintained tight control over the flow of information, with many internet websites blocked, and journalists and internet users harassed and imprisoned for the peaceful expression of opinions. The authorities made increased use of punitive forms of administrative detention, notably the Re-education through Labour system,[2] to silence critics in the lead-up to the Olympic Games.

The Justice System

Individuals who peacefully exercised their rights to freedom of expression, assembly and association remained at high risk of harassment, house arrest, arbitrary detention, and torture and other ill-treatment. Family members of human rights activists, including children, were increasingly targeted by the authorities, including being subjected to long-term house arrest and harassment by security forces. Lawyers who took on sensitive

---

1. The Uighurs are a Turkic ethnic group, most of whom live in the Xinjiang Uighur Autonomous Region under Chinese control.
2. Re-education through labor is a system of administrative detention in China used to detain people without trial for minor crimes and crimes against the state.

cases were also at risk; several had their licences suspended, and others lost their jobs. Some lawyers were specifically warned by the authorities not to take on sensitive cases, including cases of Tibetans arrested during the unrest in Tibetan areas and Falun Gong[3] practitioners.

> Chen Guangcheng, blind activist and legal adviser, continued to suffer ill-treatment in prison. He is serving a prison sentence of four years and three months after he tried to hold local officials in Shandong accountable for conducting forced abortions and sterilizations in order to enforce birth quotas. His wife, Yuan Weijing, continued to suffer police harassment, particularly in the lead-up to the Beijing Olympics, and remained under tight police surveillance.

The criminal justice system remained highly vulnerable to political interference. The courts, the prosecuting organ (procuratorate) and the police remained under the supervision of the Chinese Communist Party. The authorities continued to use broad and vaguely defined provisions of the criminal law relating to state security and "state secrets" to silence dissent and punish human rights defenders. Many of those charged under "state secrets" provisions received unfair trials and, in accordance with criminal procedure law provisions, were not given the protections afforded to other criminal suspects regarding access to legal counsel and family, and open trials.

The authorities intensified their use of administrative forms of detention which allowed police to incarcerate individuals without trial. Hundreds of thousands of individuals were in administrative detention, including in Re-education through Labour camps, where they may be detained for up to four years without trial. Secret detention centres on the outskirts of Beijing, referred to as "black jails", reportedly detained thousands of petitioners—individuals seeking redress

3. Falun Gong is a spiritual discipline founded in 1992. Its practice is strongly condemned by the Chinese government.

from central authorities for a wide variety of grievances they were unable to resolve locally—before they were forcibly returned to their home towns. Detainees in administrative detention remained at high risk of torture and other ill-treatment. In November, the UN Committee Against Torture (CAT) called upon China to "immediately abolish all forms of administrative detention".

> In June, police detained Sichuan-based human rights activist Huang Qi on suspicion of "unlawful holding of documents classified as highly secret". The reason for his detention was unclear, but appeared to be connected to his work assisting the families of five primary school pupils who died when their school buildings collapsed in the Sichuan earthquake in May [2008]. The families were seeking compensation from local officials because they believed corruption led to poor construction standards. Huang Qi was held incommunicado for over 100 days before his first meeting with a lawyer in September. In October, he refused the authorities' offer to release him on condition he gave up human rights work. He remained in detention without trial or access to his family.

Despite legal reforms, torture and other ill-treatment continued in prisons, police stations, Re-education through Labour camps, and other unofficial detention facilities. Human rights defenders, petitioners, Tibetans, Uighurs, Falun Gong practitioners, Christians, and others practising their religion in officially unsanctioned ways were at particular risk of torture and other ill-treatment by the authorities and unidentified individuals.

During the year [2008], the authorities stated their intention to increase the use of lethal injection as a "more humane" method of execution than firing squad. Amnesty International estimates a minimum of 7,000 death sentences were handed down and 1,700 executions took place. However, the authorities refused to make public national statistics on death sentences and executions and the real figure is undoubtedly higher.

In December, China voted against a UN General Assembly resolution calling for a worldwide moratorium on executions.

Freedoms of Speech and Religion

The government maintained strict control on freedom of expression. Internet users and journalists were at risk of harassment and imprisonment for addressing politically sensitive topics. Approximately 30 journalists and 50 other individuals remained in prison for posting their views on the internet.

Two weeks prior to the Olympics, the authorities established "protest zones" in three Beijing parks where people were allowed to demonstrate. However, no individuals were known to have received official permission to protest and the zones remained empty. Numerous people were detained and put under surveillance in connection with their applying for permission to protest.

The authorities unblocked a number of internet websites days before the Olympics. However, many more remained blocked. In October [2008], the authorities announced that regulations put in place in January 2007 that eased controls over foreign journalists covering the Olympics would be extended indefinitely.

The authorities questioned and harassed numerous signatories of Charter 08, which proposed a blueprint for fundamental legal and political reform in China.

Signatory Liu Xiaobo remained in detention at year's end.

Individuals who practised their religion outside officially sanctioned channels, including Christians, Muslims, Buddhists and others, faced harassment and persecution. The authorities harassed, detained and often ill-treated members of unsanctioned Christian house-churches, and confiscated or destroyed their church property. Falun Gong practitioners were among those most harshly persecuted by the government. In the run-up to the Beijing Olympics, thousands were reported to have been arrested, with hundreds imprisoned or assigned to Re-education through Labour camps and other forms of administrative detention where they were at risk of torture and other ill-treatment sometimes leading to death.

> On 25 January [2008], Yu Zhou, a well-known folk singer, graduate of Beijing University, and reportedly a Falun Gong practitioner, was arrested in Tongzhou District, Beijing, along with his wife, Xu Na, a poet and painter. On 6 February, the authorities from the Qinghe District Emergency Centre told his family that Yu Zhou had died from either diabetes or from a hunger strike, although the family maintains he was healthy at the time of his arrest. The staff at the Emergency Centre refused the family's request to view the body and for an autopsy. On 25 November, Xu Na was sentenced to three years in prison for "using a heretical organization to undermine the implementation of the law". She appealed against the sentence and is at risk of torture and other ill-treatment in detention.

Tibet and Surrounding Areas

Tibetan-populated areas of China remained tightly sealed off from outside scrutiny following unrest in March [2008]. After the initial few days, protests were largely peaceful. However, the authorities reported that 21 people had been killed by violent protesters and overseas Tibetan organizations reported that over 100 Tibetans had been killed. While Chinese authorities announced that over 1,000 individuals detained in the protests had been released, overseas Tibetan organizations estimated that at least several hundred remained in detention at year's end. Exact numbers were difficult to determine because the authorities denied access to media and independent monitors. There were reports of torture and other ill-treatment in detention, in some cases resulting in death. Major monas-

Chinese Uighur Muslims

The Chinese government is directing a crushing campaign of religious repression against China's Muslim Uighurs in the name of anti-separatism and counter-terrorism. . . .

Chinese policy and law enforcement stifle religious activity and thought even in school and at home. One official document goes so far as to say that "parents and legal guardians may not allow minors to participate in religious activities."

"The worldwide campaign against terrorism has given Beijing the perfect excuse to crack down harder than ever in Xinjiang," said Brad Adams, Asia director for Human Rights Watch. . . .

The Uighurs, a Turkic-speaking minority of some 8 million people, whose traditional homeland lies in the oil-rich Xinjiang Uighur Autonomous Region in northwest China, have become increasingly fearful for their cultural survival and traditional way of life in the face of an intensive internal migration drive that has witnessed the arrival of more than 1.2 million ethnic Chinese settlers over the past decade. Many Uighurs desire greater autonomy than is currently allowed; some wish for a separate state, although there is little recent evidence of violent rebellion.

Human Rights Watch, April 10, 2005.

teries and nunneries were reported to remain under virtual lock-down. Local authorities renewed the "Patriotic Education" campaign which required Tibetans to participate in collective criticism sessions of the Dalai Lama and to sign written denunciations against him. Tibetan members of the Chinese

Communist Party were also targeted by this campaign, including being forced to remove their children from Tibet exile community schools, where they were obtaining religious education.

> Paltsal Kyab, a Tibetan from Sichuan province, died on 26 May, five weeks after he had been detained by police in connection with the protests. Aged around 45, Paltsal Kyab had been present at a protest march on 17 March in Charo township in Ngaba (Ch:Aba) county. His family was not given permission to visit him in detention and had no news of his situation until 26 May when two Charo township leaders informed them of his death. When family members went to claim his body, they found it bruised and covered with blister burns, discovering later that he had internal injuries. The police told them that he had died of an illness, although relatives claimed he was healthy when first detained.

The Uighur Muslim population in the Xinjiang Uighur Autonomous Region (XUAR) in northwest China faced intensified persecution. The authorities used a series of violent incidents, allegedly linked to terrorists, to launch a sweeping crackdown. According to official media, almost 1,300 people were arrested during the year on terrorism, religious extremism or other state security charges, and 1,154 were formally charged and faced trials or administrative punishments. On 14 August, Wang Lequan, Party Secretary of the XUAR, announced a "life and death" struggle against Uighur "separatism".

> Ablikim Abdiriyim, the son of exiled Uighur human rights activist, Rebiya Kadeer, remained in Baijiahu prison on a charge of "separatism", for which he was sentenced to nine years in prison in April 2007. On 6 December 2007, during the first permitted visit since his detention, his family found him to be in extremely poor health. Prison authorities attributed this to a heart condition, suggesting that it could deteriorate further if he refused to "cooperate" or "admit his

guilt". Despite ongoing requests from his family, the authorities refused to grant him parole for medical treatment.

Local authorities maintained tight control over religious practice, including prohibiting all government employees and children under the age of 18 from worshipping at mosques.

One hundred and sixty Uighur children, aged between eight and 14, who had been living and studying in a Hui [a Chinese ethnic group] Muslim area of Yunnan province, were reportedly arrested by police sent by the Public Security Bureau in the XUAR. They were brought to Urumqi and held in Baijiahu prison. Ten of the children were reportedly released after their parents paid 20,000 Yuan ($3,140). Those who could not pay were told that their children would be charged with participating in "illegal religious activities".

According to reports, many people sentenced to death in the XUAR, some of whom had been given death sentences with two-year reprieves, were executed in 2008. Following domestic legal practice, death sentences with two-year reprieves can be commuted to life imprisonment if individuals exhibit good behaviour during the first two years. With the exception of one Tibetan case, the XUAR remains the only region in China where individuals are executed for political crimes.

> *"Not to talk about Chinese human rights issues is effectively blocking the [U.S.] effort . . . to solve the economic and security issues [with China]."*

Human Rights Must Be the Most Important Issue Between the United States and China

Wei Jingsheng

Wei Jingsheng is an activist in the Chinese democracy movement. In the following open letter to U.S. secretary of state Hillary Rodham Clinton, he argues that human rights is the most important issue in U.S.-China relations. Wei argues that because of a lack of democracy, China is able to exploit its own workers. This, Wei contends, contributes to runaway production, trade imbalances, environmental degradation, and indirectly to security problems. Thus, Wei maintains, the major issues between the United States and China cannot be resolved without first addressing human rights abuses.

Wei Jingsheng, "Open Letter from Wei Jingsheng to US Secretary of State Hillary Clinton," Wei Jingsheng Foundation, February 21, 2009. Copyright © 2009 Wei Jingsheng Foundation. Reproduced by permission, www.weijingsheng.org.

As you read, consider the following questions:

1. During which presidential administration was the author rescued from China?

2. According to Wei, what was the root cause of the economic crisis of the late first decade of the twenty-first century?

3. According to the author, where has criticism of Secretary Clinton come from?

R espected Secretary of State [Hillary Rodham] Clinton,

I am a political prisoner rescued from China during President William Clinton's term.[1] I was fortunate to be invited to the White House to meet with then President Clinton, as well as to be introduced to you by President Vaclav Havel of the Czech Republic during a banquet hosted by him. The rescued political prisoners like us, and the Chinese people during that era, had all appreciated very much the human rights diplomacy of the USA. We have cheered for its success, as well as sighed for its shortcomings. We are actively seeking the reasons for the shortcomings. When there is inappropriate wording, please forgive us.

Unfortunately we saw some huge mistakes during President Clinton's Administration. The first was the unlinking of Chinese human rights from trade issues, and the second was forcefully pushing the Congress to offer PNTR (i.e. Most Favored Nation status)[2] to China. The result was that it not only reduced America's international prestige and damaged the democratic progress in China, but also brought disastrous long-term results for America's own economy and employment opportunities. According to the data released by the US

1. President William (Bill) Clinton is married to Hillary Clinton, who was First Lady when she met Wei.
2. Most favored nation status grants a nation trade advantages with the United States.

Labor Conditions in China

A year and a half after a landmark labor law took effect in China, experts say conditions have actually deteriorated in southern China's export-oriented factories, which produce many of America's less expensive retail goods.

With China's exports reeling and unemployment rising because of the global slowdown, there is growing evidence that factories are ignoring or evading the new law, and that the government is reluctant to enforce it.

Government critics say authorities fear that a crackdown on violators could lead to mass layoffs and even social unrest. . . .

But workers are fighting back. [In early June 2009], the government said Chinese courts were trying to cope with a soaring number of labor disputes, apparently from workers emboldened by the promise of the new contract labor law.

David Barboza, New York Times, *June 22, 2009.*

government, during this period, the US trade deficit with China grew rapidly by a factor of 10 to more than 300 billion dollars annually, accumulating a total of more than 2 trillion dollars.

Generally, people expected you to make a correction to this important historic mistake after you became the Secretary of State [in 2009] and to re-emphasize the human rights issue in China. However, from what you said and did during your visit to China this time [in February 2009], it was not the case. Using the words of the Chinese Communist government's Internet agents, the human rights diplomacy of the USA has come to its end.

Human Rights Are a U.S. Interest

Is it true that there is no relationship between Chinese human rights and the US interests? That is not so. Although the trigger for the economic crisis [of 2008–2009] in the USA was in the financial sector, the root cause was the trade imbalance, especially the huge trade deficit with China that has effectively destroyed the real economy in the USA. The [Barack] Obama Administration has been mobilizing Americans to overcome the difficulty and revive the real economy, as the prerequisite to tide over the current economic crisis. The real prerequisite of this policy is to block the huge loophole of the foreign trade deficit. Otherwise, billions of dollars from the economic stimulus package will simply become the profit of the multinational companies and the Chinese government.

How was this huge US trade deficit to China formed? The most important reason out of the many was due to unfair and unequal trade with China. China is not a free market economy but a totalitarian country under one party dictatorship. The Chinese Communist government controls China's trade. Chinese workers do not have rights to protect their own interests. The government controls the Chinese media. It is exactly these human rights problems that result in the unfair and unequal trade, producing the abnormal trade deficit, tipping the economy of the developed countries, and finally ending with the current economic crisis. The imbalanced economic development in China has also resulted in the global energy crisis and environment pollution, and indirectly threatens the global security. All of these issues were of your attention during your trip to China, yet you have failed to put human rights as your top priority.

Thus, not to talk about Chinese human rights issues is effectively blocking the effort by the Obama Administration to solve the economic and security issues. I do not think that fits your responsibility as the US Secretary of State, or your purpose of visiting China now. There is a huge wave of criticism of your conduct related to your China visit this time, both inside China and Overseas, as well as in English and in Chinese. This failure has severely damaged the image of the Obama Administration, resulting in a huge misunderstanding of the US government, and also severely harming Americans' expectation of President Obama. I wish that you would take effective steps to remedy that.

If you think that there is a need, I am willing to discuss the related issues with you further.

Best wishes that your work will be productive and successful.

Periodical Bibliography

The following articles have been selected to supplement the diverse views presented in this chapter.

BBC News Online	"China 'Will Not Have Democracy,'" March 9, 2009. http://news.bbc.co.uk.
James A. Dorn	"China's Dilemma," Cato Institute, April 19, 2006. www.cato.org.
Gary Feuerberg	"China's Human Rights Lawyers Face Major Obstacles," *Epoch Times*, July 15, 2009. www.theepochtimes.com.
John Gittings	"China's Uighur Conundrum," *Guardian* (Manchester, U.K.), July 7, 2009. www.guardian.co.uk.
Zlatica Hoke	"Uighurs: China's Muslim Minority Claims to Be Marginalized in Its Ancestral Homeland," *VOA News*, July 22, 2009. www.voanews.com.
Thomas Kleiber	"The Twin Betrayals of the Olympics in 1936 and 2008," *Epoch Times*, May 12, 2008. www.theepochtimes.com.
Alison Klyaman	"Wu Qing, Chinese People's Deputy Also Advocate for Civil Rights," *VOA News*, July 22, 2009. www.voanews.com.
John Lee	"Putting Democracy on Hold," Center for Independent Studies, n.d. (2007). www.cis.org.au.
Ying Ma	"China's Stubborn Anti-democracy," *Policy Review*, February/March 2007. www.hoover.org.
New York Times	"China Terrorizes Tibet," March 18, 2008. www.nytimes.com.

OPPOSING VIEWPOINTS® SERIES

CHAPTER 2

How Is China Handling Its Economic Challenges?

Chapter Preface

Hong Kong is one of China's largest trading ports and financial centers. It is also quasi-independent. For many years, Hong Kong was a British possession and, therefore, a democracy. In 1997, in accordance with prior agreements, it was transferred to China. Now Hong Kong's foreign affairs and defense policy are controlled by China, though it retains its own legal and political system, as well as its own currency.

Hong Kong's standard of living remains much higher than in other parts of China. Still, in integrating with China, Hong Kong has faced economic adjustments. It experienced an economic slowdown directly after the handover because of uncertainty and other factors. In addition, Frank Yu, general manager of the Multimedia Innovation Centre of Hong Kong's Polytechnic University, noted on the Web site Frank Yu's China Recon in 2002 that "before the opening of China, Hong Kong benefited from being the main interface into communist China." As Hong Kong has become more integrated with China, however, and as China has itself expanded economically, Hong Kong's special status as the economic link between West and East has been called into question. In March 2008, for example, the Chinese government declared its intention to make Shanghai an international financial and shipping hub by the year 2020. According to the *Economist*, in an article on June 4, 2009, "Hong Kong's political and business leaders gasped at this frontal assault on the enclave's cherished role as an international gateway to the mainland."

The rapid changes in China's economy have had benefits for Hong Kong too, however. As a financial center, Hong Kong was badly hit by the global financial crisis of 2008 and 2009. China, which was not as badly damaged, issued bonds in Hong Kong in an effort to help alleviate the credit crisis that made it hard for banks to borrow or lend.

For China itself, the greater ties with Hong Kong have been one part of the nation's growing economic power. Hong Kong is a major investor in the rest of China, and so it helps to counterbalance China's heavy reliance on foreign investment and exports. In addition, U.S. consul general Michael Klosson noted in a speech to the Asia Society in Houston in 2001 that "a vibrant Hong Kong helps China's prosperity and pride by being a world-class, international city that provides talent, capital, and experience to the mainland." The transfer of Hong Kong to China, in other words, has been one part of the expansion that has, in the last decades, made China a global economic power.

> "With China's 1.3 billion consumers
> having an average rate of savings in
> excess of 30% and essentially no debt,
> ... China's domestic economy can be
> sustained indefinitely."

The Global Recession Did Not Weaken China's Economy

Jeff Nielson

Jeff Nielson is a Canadian writer/editor for Bullion Bulls Canada, a Web site covering the precious metals markets. In the following viewpoint, he argues that the Chinese economy remains strong and that it should continue to grow indefinitely. Though China has seen slowing growth in industrial production and in its largest cities, it has made up for this through growth in second-tier cities and through an expansion of its service economy. Nielson claims that media outlets that deny China's growth are propagandistically trying to increase confidence in the American economy.

As you read, consider the following questions:

1. According to Nielson, which economy has been the most popular target of U.S. propagandists?

Jeff Nielson, "Chinese Economy Is Strong, Despite Media Claims," *Seeking Alpha*, June 10, 2009. Reproduced by permission.

2. According to Nielson, on what did the *Wall Street Journal* base its argument that China's economy was weaker than it appeared?

3. According to China's spokesperson and to Nielson, what offset the 20 percent decline in international trade?

Not all the efforts of the U.S. propaganda-machine are directed at generating false-hope in the U.S. economy and warping economic statistics beyond recognition. A large component of this campaign is to undermine confidence in *other* economies—in order to try to make investing in U.S. assets appear to be the least-worst alternative.

Of course, there is no need for the U.S. propaganda-machine to attempt to undermine the Canadian economy. With a Goldman Sachs Stooge in charge of our central bank,[1] and a U.S. lap-dog for a Prime Minister [Stephen Harper], those two have managed to undermine confidence in the *Canadian* economy—unassisted.

Anti-China Propaganda

However, with China being the new, economic growth-engine for the global economy, and with no Goldman Sachs Stooges strategically appointed in *that* government, China has been the *2nd* most-popular target of U.S. propagandists—right after Europe.

While I'm a little late in seeing this, the Chinese government publicly rebutted a recent (May 15th [2009]) 'hatchet-job' by the *Wall Street Journal*, which selectively plucked a couple of pieces of data, and then 'spun' a story suggesting that China's economy was much weaker than people thought. It actually had the audacity to imply that *China* was falsifying statistics.

1. Goldman Sachs is a large U.S. investment bank. Many high-level government officials have worked at Goldman Sachs, including then treasury secretary Henry Paulson. The head of the central bank, Ben Bernanke, did not work at Goldman Sachs.

China Stronger than the West

There are *three, HUGE differences* between China's economy (and consumers) compared to anemic, Western economies.

1. Chinese people have a HUGE pool of savings—as the Chinese people have *always* had one of the highest savings rates in the world. . . .

2. China's economy has *never stopped* GROWING. . . .

3. China's government ALSO has a huge surplus, meaning it was able to engage in *rapid, massive stimulus of the economy*—without going into debt.

Jeff Nielson,
www.bullionbullscanada.com, April 9, 2009.

With the United States being the greatest statistical liar the world has ever seen, this accusation by the *Wall Street Journal* certainly evokes a reminder of that old saying that "people who live in glass houses shouldn't throw stones."

The Chinese retort came from its "National Bureau of Statistics," in the form of a question-and-answer interview. The Chinese representative quickly got to the point:

> To my regret, the views expressed . . . lack evidence and some views are the conclusions made by private consulting services. We believe that it is not serious for an international agency to do it this way.

To people familiar with China's subdued manner and penchant for understatement, this is strong language—just short of calling the *Wall Street Journal* article a deliberate and disingenuous attack (i.e. propaganda).

The *WSJ* disinformation based its smear on essentially three pieces of data: a small drop in electricity consumption, a low rate of *increase* in energy consumption, and a large drop in trade (i.e. exports).

China dealt with the energy number first. The spokesman pointed out that there was nothing inconsistent about reporting a 6.1% increase in GDP [gross domestic product] coinciding with a 3% rise in energy consumption (especially given the commitment of the Chinese government to improving energy efficiency as one means of combating its severe environmental problems).

He then went on to address the small decline in electricity consumption.

> We think that there are two elements to explain it. The first one was a big change in the industrial structure in 1Q09 [the first quarter of 2009] due to the rapid growth of the tertiary sector [that is, the service sector], a sector that usually has less consumption of electricity. The tertiary sector made a year-on-year [year-over-year] growth of 7.4%, 2.1 percentage points higher than the secondary sector [industrial sector], and its contribution to the GDP grew from 42.7% a year earlier to 44.1%, already over-taking the industrial sector. By contrast, the value added [sales tax] of the industrial sector contributed 46% in 1Q08 [the first quarter of 2008] and 44.1% in 1Q09.

For those who might think this is some arbitrary distinction, invented solely to obfuscate the data, think again. The Chinese government has regularly used such distinctions to categorize its economy (and its cities).

Rebalancing, Not Slowing

Indeed, the *Financial Times* did a series of features on the evolution of China's economy, specifically pointing to the rapid growth of "second-tier" and "third-tier" cities, versus the "first-tier" or primary cities—which refers to the large, coastal hubs which are focused on exports and international trade.

I wrote several pieces myself on this evolution, . . . to demonstrate how the 20+% growth of China's *domestic* economy was offsetting the declines in China's exports.

The Chinese spokesman then continued on in greater detail about how the rebalancing of China's economy has led to less energy-intensive industries outperforming the less-efficient users of energy.

Then, to "kick some sand" in the face of the *Wall Street Journal* he cited a U.S. example, "*U.S. electricity use dropped by 3.6% in 2001, while its GDP grew by 0.8%.*" This was followed by a parallel example from Japan, and then two counter-examples, where Japan and Korea reported *declines* in their GDP, but sharp *growth* in electricity consumption.

Finally, the spokesman dealt with the 20% decline in trade which coincided with the 6.1% rise in GDP, by pointing to exactly what I had previously written about myself: the 20+% growth in China's domestic economy. . . .

With China's *1.3 billion* consumers having an *average* rate of savings in excess of 30% and essentially *no debt*, this rate of increase in China's domestic economy *can be sustained indefinitely*.

In short, China has had little difficulty in mounting a credible defense of *its own* economic statistics. I *strongly doubt* that we will ever witness a U.S. government spokesman attempting a similarly detailed defense of U.S. economic "statistics." The number of *additional* lies which would have to be constructed to engage in such an exercise would obviously be counter-productive—merely highlighting the extremely dubious validity of every statistical calculation produced by the U.S.

> *"There is an increased risk that China will grow only in the 5% to 6% range year-on-year in 2009, about half its average growth of the previous five years, and well below potential."*

The Global Recession Weakened China's Economy

Nouriel Roubini

Nouriel Roubini is a professor at the Stern Business School at New York University and chairman of Roubini Global Economics. In the following viewpoint, he argues that the economic crisis badly hurt Chinese growth. Roubini says that Chinese growth seems set to resume at a slower pace than previously, but he argues that a full recovery will not occur until there is a global recovery and the rest of the world again starts buying Chinese goods. Even then, Roubini argues, the U.S.-China trade that fueled China's remarkable expansion may not be what it was before the crisis.

Nouriel Roubini, "The Outlook for China's Economy," *Forbes.com*, April 9, 2009. Copyright © 2009 Forbes LLC. Reprinted by permission of Forbes.com.

As you read, consider the following questions:

1. According to Roubini, Chinese growth calculated on a quarter-to-quarter basis may have been as low as what in the second half of 2008?

2. According to the author, when is the global economy likely to recover, in 2009 or 2010?

3. Does Roubini think that China is in a better or worse position than its emerging market peers?

China, the world's second largest economy by purchasing power parity[1] contributed over 10% to global economic output in 2007 and 2008 and is thus a key part of any recovery of the global economy. China faced a severe deceleration of growth in the second half of 2008 based on a number of indicators: GDP, production of electricity, the Purchasing Managers' Index (PMI),[2] weakness of auto sales, a fall in residential home sales, manufacturing data and falling imports and exports. In fact, calculated on a quarter-by-quarter basis like most other countries, Chinese growth (which is reported only on a year-on-year basis) was practically zero and even negative by some private sector estimates.

Slow Recovery

However, there are greater signs of economic recovery in March [2009] from the depths of the fourth quarter of 2008, and most forward-looking indicators suggest that from the second to the fourth quarter of 2009, growth will accelerate relative to the dismal fourth quarter of 2008 and weak first quarter of 2009.

In particular, economic data for China (including loan growth, the PMI, recovery in residential sales volume—if not

---

1. Purchasing power parity means that figures are adjusted to take account of exchange rates.
2. GDP is gross domestic product; it and PMI are both economic indicators.

prices—and public investment) do point to a stabilization or even slight improvement; but I still see risks that Chinese growth will be well below the government target of 8%, and even below the 6.5% level that the IMF [International Monetary Fund] and World Bank are predicting—a figure of 5% to 6% seems more likely.

The more optimistic outlook for Chinese growth would require a recovery in the global economy, especially the U.S., in the second half of 2009, a development that seems more likely to come in 2010. It seems too soon to point to an economic recovery, particularly in the absence of a rebound in demand from the G-3 economies (the U.S., European Union and Japan) that absorb most of Chinese exports.

There are other risks to this scenario. First, the Chinese policy stimulus could turn out to be insufficient, and further stimulus could be delayed. Second, if a "drugged" recovery— via easy money, loose fiscal policy and easy credit—leads to further over-capacity (of which there is some evidence), it could result in rising non-performing loans, falling profits or rising losses.

Given the collapse of external demand, exports are now in free fall, while the policies that will eventually lead to greater consumption have been woefully slow to be implemented. The job of lifting domestic demand is mostly in the hands of an aggressive ("pro-active" in their terms) fiscal policy and a more easy ("moderately easy" in their terms) monetary and credit policy.[3] Although government-linked investment rose sharply beginning in February 2009, private-sector capital expenditure (mostly financed via retained earnings) is likely to stay weak in 2009, given sharp profit declines.

Furthermore, although indicators of private consumption like retail sales have remained relatively robust, they are growing at a slower pace compared to the second half of 2008. The

---

3. An aggressive fiscal policy means more government spending. An easy monetary policy means lower interest rates.

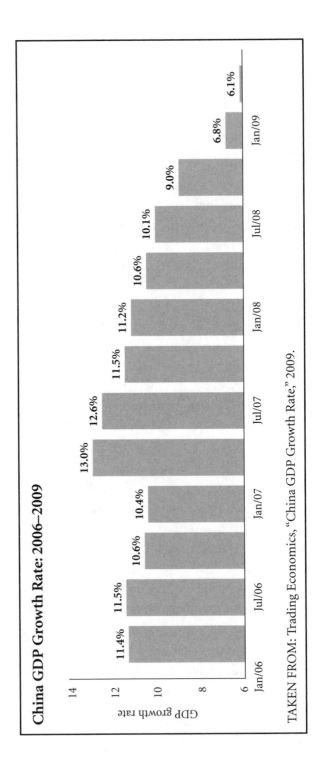

China GDP Growth Rate: 2006–2009

TAKEN FROM: Trading Economics, "China GDP Growth Rate," 2009.

extent of job losses and falling incomes as well as negative consumer confidence may slow consumption further going forward, particularly in urban areas, despite government incentives.

Despite the fact that China's aggressive policy response included monetary easing, a scaling up of bank lending and a particularly aggressive scaling up of government investment to offset the contraction in private demand, there is an increased risk that China will grow only in the 5% to 6% range year-on-year in 2009, about half its average growth of the previous five years, and well below potential. Such a growth rate would increase pressures on China's government, as the hard landing has been accompanied by job losses and factory closures as well as implying that Chinese commodity demand could continue to be lower than recent trends.

The World Has Changed

There are signs that the Chinese government is increasingly front-loading its investment and backstopping bond issuances of cash-strapped regional and local governments that are being expected to provide their own contributions. And although implementation has been slow, the government has tweaked its spending to increase allocations to social welfare programs. China is also taking the time to allocate spending to meet longer-term goals, including increasing the share of renewable fuels in its energy mix. However, the finance ministry's implicit 3% of GDP bound for its fiscal deficit means that revenue shortfalls might limit additional spending should it be needed in 2010. Nonetheless, China's domestic savings, its low debt and the fact that it is still attracting foreign direct investment, albeit at a slower pace than 2008, imply that it is better positioned than many of its emerging-market peers, in part because it can raise funds domestically to finance its deficits.

The structural reasons for high Chinese savings rates still persist. And with the Chinese yuan having returned to its implicit peg to the U.S. dollar, Chinese reserve accumulation and purchase of U.S. assets could again be quite strong in 2009. However, lower net hot money inflows could contribute to keep the pace of reserve accumulation below the one displayed in 2008.

But the gap between a very weak U.S. and global economy and the Chinese growth target of 8% for 2009 is wide, and given the sluggish outlook for the U.S. and global economy, China may continue to grow below potential in 2010. There is also another important caveat: Even once the U.S. economy recovers, it will rely less on consumption and imports and more on an improvement in net exports. The world where the U.S. was the consumer of first and last resort—spending more than its income and running an ever larger current account deficit[4]—and where China was the producer of first and last resort, spending less than its income and running ever larger current account surpluses, is changing.

---

4. The current account is part of the balance of trade. So a current account deficit is essentially a trade deficit.

"What Congress needs to be told is: free trade [with China] is mutually beneficial."

Free Trade with China Benefits Both China and the United States

James A. Dorn

James A. Dorn is a China specialist at the libertarian Cato Institute. In the following viewpoint, he argues that nations benefit not only from exports, but from imports as well. U.S. consumers gain from cheap imports, he says. In addition, Dorn notes Chinese imports are responsible for only a very small number of job losses in the U.S. Dorn further argues that it would be unethical to raise tariffs on China in violation of international agreements. China's trade policies have been improving, Dorn says, and the United States should engage in dialogue to encourage further improvements.

As you read, consider the following questions:

1. According to Dorn, when did China unilaterally liberalize its trading regime?

James A. Dorn, "Ties That Blind," *South China Morning Post*, May 1, 2007. Reproduced by permission.

2. According to Daniel Griswold, as cited by the author, what percent of overall U.S. job displacement is due to imports from China?

3. According to Dorn, China has made progress on market access and rules-based issues, but needs to do better at enforcing what?

A crescendo of voices on Capitol Hill is calling for retaliation against China for "cheating" on its trade commitments and for undervaluing its currency. Senator Byron Dorgan, a Democrat from North Dakota, has even introduced a bill to end normal trading relations with China. The presumption is China must be "cheating"—and doing so at the expense of US jobs—because the American bilateral trade deficit with China continues to reach new highs. To "level the playing field" and correct the trade imbalance, which reached US$233 billion [in 2006], Congress must retaliate with protectionist measures.

Bad Logic

False logic underlies this vision of US-China trade. Trade is too often seen as a zero-sum game—one party wins; the other loses—with the prize being a trade surplus. That mercantilist[1] attitude, which [Scottish philosopher] David Hume in 1758 called "a narrow and malignant opinion", accounts for a large amount of the China-bashing in Washington today. By focusing on producers who may have been harmed by trade rather than on consumers who benefit, Congress commits the same fallacy of composition that Hume exposed. Moreover, by failing to recognise the widespread benefits of trade for all nations, protectionists have lost sight of the liberal idea best expressed by Hume that "where an open communication is

---

1. Mercantilism is an economic theory that holds that nations grow in prosperity by exporting more than they import.

preserved among nations, it is impossible but the domestic industry of every one must receive an increase from the improvements of the others".

If China had not unilaterally liberalised its state-controlled trading regime after 1978, both China and the global economy would surely be much worse off today. Likewise, if the US is overly zealous in restricting Chinese goods imports, the long-term impact will be to lower the growth of US exports to China and a reduction in the wealth of both nations.

What Congress needs to be told is: free trade is mutually beneficial—consumers gain regardless of why imports are cheap; the purpose of trade is not to create jobs but to create wealth; and that the balance of payments must always balance because of double-entry bookkeeping—a current account deficit must be offset by a capital account surplus.[2]

All the protectionist hyperbole diverts attention from the significant progress China has made in its transition from a planned to a market economy, the increase in economic and personal freedom the Chinese have acquired, and the enormous benefits to consumers from the availability of cheap Chinese imports.

No One Forced to Trade

The truth is that no one is forced to trade with China. As Minister of Commerce Bo Xilai noted in responding to US protectionist threats: "If they [American businesses] could not make money doing business with China, they would not have been doing it."

Daniel Griswold, director of the Cato Institute's Centre for Trade Policy Studies, estimates that annual net job losses in the US due to imports from China "account for only about 1 per cent of overall job displacement". Yet industries that feel the pain of those losses will find it expedient to lobby for protection at the expense of American consumers.

2. The current account is part of the balance of trade, so a current account deficit is essentially a trade deficit.

Jobs Abroad = Jobs at Home

There is no evidence that expanding employment at U.S.-owned affiliates comes at the expense of overall employment by parent companies back home in the United States. In fact ... foreign and domestic operations tend to complement each other and expand together.... More activity and sales abroad often require the hiring of more managers, accountants, lawyers, engineers, and production workers at the parent company.

Consider Caterpillar Inc., the Peoria, Illinois–based company known for making giant earth-moving equipment. From 2005 through 2007, the company enjoyed booming global sales because of strong growth in overseas markets, especially those with resources extracted from the ground. According to the company's 2007 annual report, Caterpillar earned 63 percent of its sales revenue abroad, including $1 billion in sales in China alone. As a result, Caterpillar ramped up employment at its overseas affiliates during that time from 41,238 to 50,788, an increase of almost 10,000 workers. During that same three-year period, the company expanded its domestic employment from 43,878 to 50,545, a healthy increase of 6,667.

Daniel T. Griswold,
Center for Trade Policy Studies,
January 13, 2009. www.freetrade.org.

The US policy of engagement has worked relatively well, as has China's policy of "peaceful development". It will take time for China to meet all its World Trade Organisation obligations. There has been much progress on market access and rules-based issues, but much remains to be done on enforcing intellectual property rights.

To cheat requires intentionally breaking agreements one has made in good faith. China has never agreed to float its currency[3] but is moving in that direction. Yet Democrat Senator Charles Schumer and Republican Senator Lindsey Graham have repeatedly threatened to impose punitive tariffs on Chinese imports unless the yuan is allowed to appreciate significantly against the US dollar.

Even though US Treasury Secretary Henry Paulson has initiated a strategic economic dialogue to promote engagement, he feels that he needs to instruct China on what is in its best interest, with an implicit threat of retaliation if Beijing moves too slowly. In recent testimony before the Committee on Banking, Housing, and Urban Affairs, Mr Paulson stated: "China must live up to its WTO [World Trade Organization] commitments. It must protect and vigorously enforce intellectual property rights. It must increasingly open its markets to foreign competition—for its own good as well as for ours. And it must introduce greater transparency in regulation and observe the rule of law."

The need to preserve "an open communication" among all nations is still of vital importance. When Mr Paulson meets Vice-Premier Wu Yi and the Chinese delegation ... in Washington for the next round of the strategic economic dialogue, he should emphasise the basic principle of unilateral free trade that Hume understood and that has made Hong Kong rich.

---

3. A floating currency is one whose price is established entirely by market forces; that is, by how much people are willing to pay for it. In contrast, a fixed currency has a price established by the government bank. China has in general kept the price of its currency artificially low, which makes its exports cheaper abroad.

> *"Our imports from China continue to outstrip our exports by more than five to one, making this by far our most imbalanced trade relationship with any major trading partner."*

Free Trade with China Benefits China but Hurts the United States

James Parks

James Parks is a journalist and a member of the AFL-CIO staff. The AFL-CIO is a federation of fifty-six national and international labor unions. In the following viewpoint, Parks argues that the enormous trade deficit with China hurts U.S. workers. Parks contends that the deficit contributes to the loss of U.S. manufacturing jobs, as more and more products are produced in China and that to solve this problem, the United States should put tariffs on Chinese goods. The United States should also encourage China to improve conditions for Chinese workers and stop artificially lowering the price of its currency, a practice that helps lower the price of Chinese exports, Parks maintains.

James Parks, "Growing U.S. Trade Deficit with China Fuels Nation's $2.5 Billion Daily Fix," AFL-CIO Now Blog, May 3, 2006. Reproduced by permission.

As you read, consider the following questions:

1. According to Robert Baugh, as cited by Parks, what is the largest U.S. export to China?

2. According to Robert Scott, as cited by the author, how much does the United States need to borrow every day to finance its deficit?

3. How many manufacturing jobs did the United States lose in 2005, according to Parks?

The Chinese government is flouting its international obligations—and no nation is holding that government accountable. As a result, the United States has a trade deficit of $900 billion—$201 billion with China alone, the largest deficit in U.S. history with one country. That deficit has cost 410,000 U.S. jobs and job opportunities in the past two years [2004–2006] alone, according to the Economic Policy Institute (EPI).

Action Needed Now

When the first quarter trade figures come out later this month [May 2006], many economists expect the deficit with China to continue to grow sharply—it jumped up by 34 percent in the past quarter. One forecaster says the deficit with China could jump by nearly 50 percent, to a whopping $300 billion by year's end.

Testifying last month before the U.S.-China Economic and Security Review Commission, Robert Baugh, executive director of the AFL-CIO Industrial Union Council, laid out the case for immediate action to thwart China's growing threat to America's economy:

> It is a sad but true fact that empty cargo containers are our largest export to China. Our imports from China continue to outstrip our exports by more than five to one, making this by far our most imbalanced trade relationship with any major trading partner. Meanwhile, the United States has lost almost 3 million manufacturing jobs since 2001.

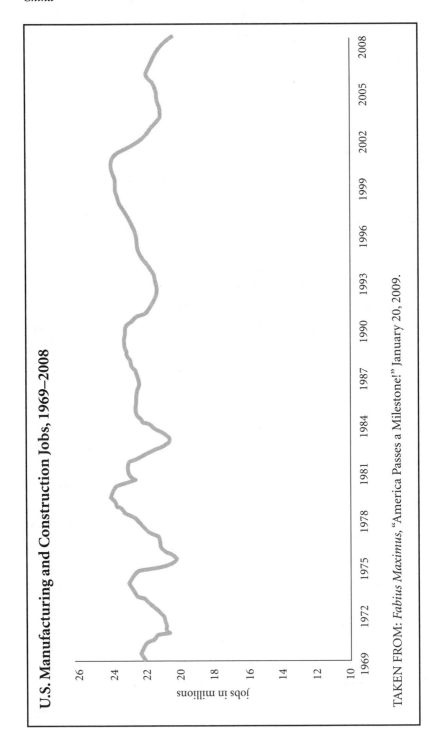

U.S. Manufacturing and Construction Jobs, 1969–2008

jobs in millions

1969 1972 1975 1978 1981 1984 1987 1990 1993 1996 1999 2002 2005 2008

TAKEN FROM: *Fabius Maximus*, "America Passes a Milestone!" January 20, 2009.

While many factors contributed to this devastating job loss, it is clear that the Chinese government's manipulation of its currency,[1] violation of international trade rules, and egregious repression of its citizens' fundamental democratic and human rights are key contributors to an unfair competitive advantage.

Unfortunately, to date, the U.S. government has failed to act effectively to stem the job losses resulting from the burgeoning U.S. trade deficit with China. The [George W.] Bush administration has refused concrete action to ensure that the Chinese government lives up to its international obligations on trade, currency manipulation and human rights. President Bush has denied American businesses and workers the import relief they are entitled to under the law, and he has taken positions at the World Trade Organization (WTO) that will only worsen our trade relationship with China.

A growing trade deficit would be especially dangerous for the U.S. economy, says EPI economist Robert Scott. Here's the reason: Last year's overall account deficit (which measures the traditional trade deficit in goods and services plus payments to foreign investors) equaled 7 percent of the nation's gross domestic product, a new record, and is rising at an annual rate of $900 billion.

Too Much Debt

That means the United States is buying about 7 percent more from foreign countries than it is producing. It needs to borrow about $2.5 billion *every day* in foreign capital to finance this deficit, Scott says. At that rate, our borrowing would wipe out Bill Gates' entire fortune in less than two months.

While Gates may not have to worry about the deficit, the average working person does. The $900 billion deficit is taking away production that could provide as many as 9 million jobs, according to EPI. The loss of jobs caused by the deficit means

1. China keeps the price of its currency low, which makes its exports cheaper.

"people are being pushed out of good paying manufacturing jobs and into restaurant jobs paying minimum wage or a little more without benefits," Scott says. The manufacturing sector has lost 3 million jobs over the past five years, including 81,000 jobs in 2005, as the manufacturing trade deficit has continued to expand.

Just as carrying huge debts is bad for your household budget, the same is true for our economy.

As Scott said back in February [2007] when last quarter figures came out:

> You can't keep borrowing $900 billion a year. China, Japan and Korea keep buying up our debt because they depend on our imports. The problem comes when other investors realize that the dollar will have to crash [drop in value] (to stabilize the world's financial markets). Then the smart investors will move all their money offshore. That will create a tsunami that no one can stop.

President George W. Bush had an opportunity during the recent summit with China's President Hu Jintao to pressure him to lower the trade deficit. But Bush let the Chinese leader slip out of any firm commitments. So members of Congress on both sides and working people are taking the lead to reduce the dangerous trade deficit. Sens. Charles Schumer (D-N.Y.) and Lindsey Graham (R-S.C.) are sponsoring legislation that would impose across-the-board penalty tariffs of 27.5 percent on Chinese goods unless the Chinese stop the practice of undervaluing their currency.

In 2004, the AFL-CIO filed a petition calling on the Bush administration to take immediate action to impose trade remedies against China and negotiate a binding agreement to reduce the trade remedies if China enforces workers' rights. The administration rejected the petition, but the AFL-CIO union movement is set to demand the Bush administration take concrete and immediate steps to press for workers' rights in China and to value its currently undervalued currency at a more accurate rate, a move that could go a long way toward reducing the trade deficit with China.

| "Unless [the trade] imbalance is fixed,
China's long-term growth prospects are
as bleak as those of the United States."

Trade Imbalances Are Dangerous for Both the United States and China

Peter Navarro

*Peter Navarro is a professor at the Merage School of Business,
University of California–Irvine and author of* The Coming
China Wars. *In the following viewpoint, he argues that China is
keeping its currency artificially low compared with the U.S. dollar. As a result, Chinese exports have been cheap. This has resulted in cheap consumer goods in the United States and a boom
in manufacturing capacity in China. It has also, however, hurt
U.S. manufacturing capacity and jobs and made China too dependent on exports. Navarro argues that China must gradually
allow its currency to rise against the U.S. dollar for the long-
term health of both nations.*

As you read, consider the following questions:

1. According to Navarro, what is the U.S. trade deficit with China per week?

2. How has the low price of the yuan hurt China's environment, in the author's opinion?

3. According to Navarro, why would it be a bad idea to immediately decouple the yuan from the dollar?

Now that we have an economic stimulus and a bank bailout plan, the next important step in America's economic recovery is to fix its mutually destructive trade imbalance with China. That should be Secretary of State Hillary Rodham Clinton's primary mission as she visits Beijing this week [February 2009].

Any such fix must begin with the realization that China is far too dependent on selling exports to the United States, while America has lost too much of its industrial and job base.

China's Currency Undervalued

At the root of the record U.S.-China trade imbalance is China's grossly undervalued currency. Whether or not China manipulates its currency, as Treasury Secretary Timothy Geithner has charged, virtually all economists agree that the yuan is significantly undervalued relative to the dollar, to which it is pegged.[1] The result: a chronic U.S. trade deficit with China that adds up to more than $5 billion a week.

In a world of free trade characterized by floating exchange rates, such a trade imbalance could never persist. Any country that ran a chronic trade deficit would see its currency depreciate [fall in value]. To bring its trade back into balance, it would sell more exports and buy fewer imports. China, by

1. That is, the yuan's value rises and falls with the value of the dollar.

pegging its currency to the dollar, subverts this free-trade adjustment process by providing a significant subsidy to Chinese exports to the United States while slapping on a stiff implicit tariff on U.S. imports into China.

On the benefit side, the undervalued yuan has allowed American consumers to enjoy a bounty of Chinese goods at artificially low prices. The way China maintains the yuan value pegged to the dollar has kept mortgage rates low and helped subsidize American home ownership.

China's undervalued currency has, however, severely weakened the U.S. economy. We are now far too dependent on consumer-driven growth. This overconsumption is mirrored in an underinvestment in domestic manufacturing and a severely weakened industrial base incapable of generating enough good jobs at decent wages. Unless that structural imbalance is fixed, America's long-term growth prospects are bleak.

China Suffers Too

China's undervalued currency has likewise been good, but is now increasingly bad, for China. On the plus side, the fixed peg has allowed China to develop a strong industrial base. By suppressing imports, the fixed peg has likewise channeled Chinese savings into business investment and thereby rapidly accelerated China's industrial development.

The China of today, however, is far too dependent on heavily polluting manufacturing industries that exact an equally heavy environmental price. Even more important, the artificially cheap yuan has suppressed the development of China's own consumer market by reducing Chinese purchasing power. With China far too dependent on export-driven growth, it is now extremely vulnerable to the current steep decline in global export demand.

A Breaking Point

Through the quarter-century in which China has been opening to world trade, Chinese leaders have deliberately held down living standards for their own people and propped them up in the United States. This is the real meaning of the vast trade surplus—$1.4 trillion and counting, going up by about $1 billion per day—that the Chinese government has mostly parked in U.S. Treasury notes. In effect, every person in the (rich) United States has over the past two years [2006–2008] or so borrowed about $4,000 from someone in the (poor) People's Republic of China.

Neither government likes to draw attention to this arrangement, because it has been so convenient on both sides. For China, it has helped the regime guide development in the way it would like—and keep the domestic economy's growth rate from crossing the thin line that separates "unbelievably fast" from "uncontrollably inflated." For America, it has meant cheaper iPods, lower interest rates, reduced mortgage payments, a lighter tax burden. But because of political tensions in both countries, and because of the huge and growing size of the imbalance, the arrangement now shows signs of cracking apart.

James Fallows, Atlantic Monthly, *January/February 2008.*

Unless that structural imbalance is fixed, China's long-term growth prospects are as bleak as those of the United States.

While both China and the United States have reached points in their economic history where the fixed-peg system serves neither country, this does not mean U.S. policymakers should demand that China immediately decouple the yuan from the dollar and freely float its currency. If China were to let its currency float free of the dollar tomorrow, it would have to stop buying U.S. Treasury bonds, interest rates would soar and any attempt by the [Barack] Obama administration to finance either its economic stimulus or bank rescue package would be overwhelmed by chaos in global financial markets.

That said, it is dearly in the best interests of both China and the United States to mutually agree to an incremental move toward a freely floating yuan over the next four years. Such an orderly revaluing of the yuan would allow the economies of both China and the United States to make the needed adjustments without shocking the global financial system.

If China agreed to such a reform, it would not only take the single most important step possible toward defusing mounting protectionist pressures. It would also chart a new, more prosperous course toward a balanced economy driven increasingly by its own domestic growth.

> "The [U.S.] Chamber [of Commerce]
> ... asks that China's leadership take
> bolder and more effective measures to
> ... decrease ... IPR infringement."

China Must Do More to Combat Intellectual Property Piracy

U.S. Chamber of Commerce

The U.S. Chamber of Commerce is a not-for-profit business federation that advocates and lobbies on behalf of business interests. In the following viewpoint, the chamber argues that China needs to do more to combat intellectual property rights (IPR) infringements such as copyright and trademark violations. The chamber states that China has made some steps to improve enforcement, to close legal loopholes, and to make sure that government computers use legal software; however, the chamber contends, IPR violations in China continue to have a severe impact on American businesses, and China could, and should, take more aggressive steps to reduce them.

Originally published September 2006. "China's WTO Implementation and Other Issues of Importance to American Business in the U.S.-China Commercial Relationship," Washington, DC: U.S. Chamber of Commerce, 2006. Copyright © 2006 U.S. Chamber of Commerce. All rights reserved. Reprinted by permission, http://www.uschamber.com.

As you read, consider the following questions:

1. According to the Chamber of Commerce, what percentage of imported goods seized by U.S. customs come from China?

2. Why does the author say that enthusiasm for China's latest action plan must be tempered?

3. What two areas in China does the chamber identify as hotspots for IPR violations?

IPR [intellectual property rights] violations in China severely affect virtually all U.S. industries in the United States and abroad. U.S. Customs seizure statistics clearly indicate that China continues to be the largest single source of counterfeit and pirated imports into the United States. In 2005, goods imported from China into the United States that were seized for IPR reasons represented 69 percent of all such goods. During the first half of 2006, total seizures at U.S. ports of counterfeit and pirated products from China increased by 21 percent to over $34.3 million, accounting for approximately 75 percent of total seizures. Increasing levels of exports of counterfeit and pirated products from Chinese companies are seriously undermining established markets for U.S. producers not only in China, but also in many other countries. Counterfeit products made in China also continue to inflict serious risks to public health and safety worldwide.

There are signs that the central government and many regional governments are committed to dealing more proactively with counterfeiting and copyright piracy, and cooperation with industry and with IPR enforcement authorities in the United States has increased. However, increased criminal enforcement and significant reductions in the levels of piracy and counterfeiting in the market are the only true measures for determining the fulfillment of these commitments. The continuing high levels of infringement are clearly exacerbating political tensions, and play into the hands of those in the United States who are threatening to impose trade barriers on imported Chinese products.

China Making Progress

The Chinese government took important steps between 2004 and early 2006 to improve legislation on IPR protection and at the same time moderately increased the number of criminal cases against trademark counterfeiters. Recently released statistics on enforcement actions for the period between January and June 2006 suggest that police actions against pirates and counterfeiters are up, and that local Administrations for Industry & Commerce (AIC) are undertaking a high number of raids on suspected infringers of IPR. However, both the number of AIC raids and the transfers of IP cases from the administrative to the criminal system appear to be fewer than in 2005, a matter which should sound a note of concern among Chamber [of Commerce] members and policymakers in the United States and China.

The Chinese government has also begun to introduce a range of systematic changes under its Action Plan announced March 8, 2006, which should increase transparency and accountability and provide greater hope for IPR owners seeking simpler and more effective enforcement of their rights. However, over the last ten years, the Chinese government has issued multiple action plans on IPR protection that have not been effectively implemented. The enthusiasm of international stakeholders, including the Chamber, for this latest Action Plan must therefore be tempered by experience, and it is clearly necessary for foreign industry and governments to follow up closely on all of China's commitments as well as continue engagement with relevant governments on critical areas of concern which have not been addressed in the most recent Action Plan or elsewhere.

At the April 2006 meeting of the JCCT [U.S.-China Joint Commission on Commerce and Trade], Vice Premier Wu Yi pledged that *"IPR trial chambers will be open in courts across China"* and that *"50 IPR Infringement Reporting Centers will be set up in 50 key cities in China."* The Chinese government completed the establishment of these centers in late August 2006, and they may prove useful for IP owners that have in the past been confused as to the correct authority with which to file enforcement complaints. But it remains unclear whether these centers will have other functions, such as the job of intervening when difficulties arise in the course of administrative transfers to judicial authorities or with protectionism.

The PRC [People's Republic of China] also announced at the April 2006 JCCT that it had issued a notice requiring the pre-loading of legal operating system software on all computers manufactured in or imported into China as well as a notice requiring government agencies to provide adequate budget for, and the purchase of computers with pre-loaded legal software. In line with these requirements, several Chinese computer manufacturers have recently signed agreements to purchase U.S. operating system software. These announcements build upon commitments undertaken by China at the July 2005 JCCT to complete its legalization program designed to ensure that all central, provincial, and local government offices use only licensed software, and to extend this program to enterprises (including state-owned enterprises) in 2006.

China Must Do More

These important commitments underscore the central government's commitment to improve IPR protection and enforcement, and create a basis for optimism that the Chinese government will continue to achieve progress in IPR protection. However, because there has not been a substantial reduction in the scope and depth of the overall IPR problem over the last two years [2004–2006], and to ensure sustainable for-

Harry Potter in China

Even the most avid American Harry Potter fans might be surprised to find that Chinese youth may have surpassed them in the number of Harry Potter sequels they have read. Who in the US, for example, has read *Harry Potter and the Waterproof Pearl*, or *Harry Potter and the Big Funnel*? Before Potter aficionados rush out to find these rare sequels, they should know that they illustrate a major problem in Chinese Pottermania: unauthorized sequels, or fakes. . . .

These are all violations of what is called Intellectual Property Rights (IPR). Infractions of IPR are certainly not unique to China. However, their wide currency in China reveals the enormous stress rapid globalization has placed on China's political and legal infrastructure.

Jonathan F. Henderson, 2007. www.harrypotterinchina.com.

ward movement in areas where strong commitments have been made, more aggressive actions, especially in the areas of enforcement and transparency, are urgently needed.

The Chamber is particularly concerned that more attention be paid in three key areas:

First, a range of measures are required to strengthen criminal, administrative, and civil enforcement of IPR and to substantially increase deterrence. Criminal enforcement of copyrights, in particular, remains almost impossible. Some of the obstacles to enforcement are clearly based on ambiguities and gaps in China's Criminal Code, in related judicial interpretations of the Supreme People's Court, and in other legislation. Perhaps of greater concern is the lack of resources and political priority given to criminal enforcement of IPR by local governments. The Chamber regards as a positive development the recent decision by the Chinese police in Shanghai to launch an investigation into a drugs counterfeiting ring on their own initiative, rather than waiting to establish that the activities of the gang met the relevant numerical threshold for criminal liability. Meanwhile, administrative fines remain a mere cost of doing business for most infringers, and the compensation issued in most civil cases remains insufficient to cover the legal fees and investigation expenses of right holders, let alone compensate for the injury suffered.

Second, we believe additional measures to permit transparent monitoring and verification of enforcement efforts and their impact are needed, especially at provincial and local levels. Timelier issuance of detailed enforcement statistics and greater publication of enforcement efforts will help to deter offenders and identify areas where enforcement is still lacking. The Chamber will continue to commit resources to work with provincial and local governments to benchmark progress and to improve transparency of enforcement statistics. We also hope that the central government will provide provincial and local governments with even clearer guidance, legal mandates, and resources to enforce the IPR of foreign and domestic stakeholders. Moreover, enforcement authorities, including those responsible for copyright, should be required to provide copies of decisions issued following the handling of administrative actions, whether based on the complaint of the IPR owner or the government's own ex-officio actions.

Third, it is vital that the PRC government commit the funds necessary to fulfill its recent JCCT commitments. For instance, Chinese government agencies as a practical matter will be able to honor China's software government legalization commitments only if they are given the funds necessary to purchase legal software (rather than copy pirated software). Clearly, if China does commit such funds, it will need to ensure that local and provincial entities actually expend such funds toward legal software, so budgeting will have to be managed carefully. Similarly, government agencies must be given the training and tools necessary to manage their software assets and prevent illegal software from finding its way onto government computers. The PRC government should also commit IPR enforcement resources to ensure that computer manufacturers and distributors in China do in fact preinstall all PCs they sell with legal software.

Better Laws, More Enforcement

Thus, even as China committed to a variety of policy changes on IPR at the JCCT meetings in 2004, 2005, and 2006, the implementation of these commitments has been mixed, and IPR infringement remains at epidemic levels. For example, new Internet regulations have been issued to protect IPR in the digital environment, but concerns remain regarding the scope of the rights protected by the new law and vague terminology in the law that could result in significant loopholes. An effective Internet law is critically important given the rapid uptake of broadband in China, the increase in Internet piracy, and the fact that all P-2-P web sites[1] streaming broadcast content without authority are headquartered in China. The Chamber hopes that China will fulfill all of its JCCT commitments, both to the letter and in spirit.

The Chamber therefore asks that China's leadership take bolder and more effective measures to generate tangible results that will lead to true deterrence and a substantial decrease in IPR infringement, with particular attention to the level of trademark counterfeiting and copyright piracy. This will require allocation of substantially greater enforcement resources at the local levels—particularly in hotspots such as Guangzhou and Shenzhen—improved laws and regulations, careful implementation of enforcement action plans, coordi-

---

1. P-2-P, or peer-to-peer, Web sites are file-sharing sites that allow users to trade copyrighted material for free.

nation and accountability among IPR enforcement agencies, and a substantially higher level of transparency regarding the government's enforcement activities.

> "Legal and commercial tools to protect IPR march hand in hand. But the commercial means must be applied first, the law second."

Business Must Combat Chinese Intellectual Property Piracy

David Wolf

David Wolf is president and chief executive officer of Wolf Group Asia, a Beijing-based corporate advisory firm. In the following viewpoint, he argues that to combat intellectual property (IP) piracy in China, businesses must reach out to customers there. Wolf says this is more effective than turning to legal remedies. In addition, Wolf notes, when governments gain access to customers in China, they gain allies in Chinese companies, which then have an incentive to join in the battle against intellectual property piracy. Wolf also notes that each kind of IP violation presents specific problems, and each should be dealt with separately.

As you read, consider the following questions:

1. According to Wolf, in which are consumers complicit: bootleg DVDs or knockoff pharmaceuticals?

David Wolf, "Government Is Not the Solution to Chinese Piracy," *Seeking Alpha*, June 25, 2007. Reproduced by permission.

2. Which piracy issues are the most serious, in the author's opinion?

3. According to Wolf, why is it helpful to have Chinese companies be plaintiffs against Chinese IP violators?

Shaun Rein fired me a link to his recent *BusinessWeek* op/ed about how it is possible to win the [intellectual property] piracy battle. It's worth a read.

He and I are often in general agreement, and I enjoy reading his stuff. In this article, he's touching on one of my favorite themes: an economic approach to reducing the size of the piracy problem will beat a moralistic approach any day.

For the sake of advancing the argument rather than denigrating Shaun's excellent piece, I want to call out one issue that his article brings to light.

Different Solutions for Different Issues

Shaun's article is broad, covering almost the entire issue of IPR [intellectual property rights] theft in China, including pirated software, counterfeit luxury goods, knockoff pharmaceuticals, tainted food, bootleg DVDs, and fake consumer electronics. It is a perfect example of one of the unspoken reasons we have not managed to solve the IPR issue in China yet: We have collectively failed to recognize that each of the manifestations of IPR theft is a separate, distinct problem with its own causes and solutions [which] causes us to search for simple solutions.

We need to recognize that China does not have one gigantic IPR problem, but several quite large IPR issues that each need to be addressed separately.

For a simple example, let's compare bootleg DVDs and knockoff pharmaceuticals. Consumers are complicit in the first. They are unwilling victims of the second. What drives these two issues, are quite different: in the case of DVDs, it is a combination of price arbitrage[1] ("It's too expensive to buy the real thing") and failed distribution ("I want the real thing, but there's no place I can buy it"). In the case of knockoff pharmaceuticals, the problem (as I understand it) is a combination of lack of awareness, profiteering medical administrators, and a distribution system that mixes the real with the fake.

The problems are different, the solutions should be as well.

The old saw about how to eat an elephant ("one bite at a time") applies here. Fix the problem by breaking it up into its component parts. Create solutions for each type of piracy one at a time.

As an aside, we must also recognize that some piracy issues are more serious than others. Motion picture and software piracy are bad things. . . . Pirated copies of Windows VISTA and *Terminator 3* on the other hand, are not likely to kill people the way, say counterfeit aircraft parts, pharmaceuticals, or batteries might.

As we disaggregate the piracy problem, we could all start spending a little more time focusing on the parts of the issue that are potentially lethal but not quite as glamorous.

Business Must Lead

As Shaun himself appears to grant in the last paragraphs of his article, engaging on the legal/moral side does have value. There are two important qualifications to that. First, the victories Shaun cites are Chinese companies suing Chinese pirates. These cases, which cannot be framed in "us vs. them" nationalistic terms, are superb examples of why the battle in the courts is best framed with Chinese plaintiffs rather than foreign ones.

1. Arbitrage is the practice of taking advantage of a price differential.

Chinese Want Real Goods

My firm ... conducted one-on-one interviews with consumers in Shanghai, Guangzhou, and Beijing. We found that consumers prefer to buy genuine articles if they can afford to pay for them. The majority of aspiring respondents said that they are buying some real products and then completing an ensemble with fakes.

Many young women making $400 a month said that they are willing to save three months of salary to buy a thousand-dollar Gucci handbag or shoes from Bally. One 23-year-old female respondent said, "Right now I can't afford to buy a lot of real Prada or Coach, so I buy the fake items. I hope that in the future I will be able to afford the real thing, but right now I want to look the part." ...

As long as companies make an effort to develop the cachet of their brands, they do not need to worry about pirates making copies of their products.

All the signs say the situation will continue to improve as spending power rises.

Shaun Rein,
BusinessWeek, *June 20, 2007.*

Second, these victories come not to companies who abstain from full participation in the market, but those who focus first on gaining full and legitimate access to their customers in China. Apart from the fact that this makes great business sense, it recognizes an often overlooked phenomenon: when a foreign company builds access to its customers in China, it automatically enlists a host of de facto allies in its fight to defend its IPR: Chinese companies who serve as partners, suppliers, distributors, retailers, promoters, developers and the like.

Legal and commercial tools to protect IPR march hand in hand. But the commercial means must be applied first, the law second.

Hollywood, take note.

At the core of Shaun's argument—and mine—is that we have to look beyond the government for solutions. Even if the government woke up Monday morning and said "Okay, let's fix the IPR thing," they would not be able to achieve a solution via fiat [by command]. They will turn to industry—us—and say "Okay, given the limitations on our police resources, how do we create a lasting solution to the issue?"

We'd better have some smart, specific, commercial answers, and be ready to mobilize our greatest assets in each fight: the ordinary Chinese who are being hurt by each specific form of piracy. Consumers, businesses with their own IPR, filmmakers, and the companies who rely on legitimate foreign IPR or IPR-based products for their livelihood. The battle can only be won on the streets, and only then will the politically controlled police and court systems recognize the value of consistent, vigorous enforcement.

| "In China, piracy is so entrenched that even the pirates complain about it."

Chinese Intellectual Property Piracy Cannot Be Avoided

Henry Blodget

Henry Blodget is the CEO of Silicon Alley Insider, a blog about Internet business trends and research. In the following viewpoint, he points out that piracy is endemic in China. This is in part because the Chinese government benefits, and in part because Chinese consumers benefit. Blodget notes that individual companies can use legal and technical means to reduce piracy of individual products, but, especially for digital products, the overall problem is unlikely to go away.

As you read, consider the following questions:

1. According to Blodget, how much of China's gross domestic product may come from piracy?

2. What are some measures that firms can take to combat piracy, in the author's opinion?

3. According to Blodget, what kind of profit margins has Microsoft been able to earn on its products in the past?

My first evening in Beijing I was lucky enough to secure a meeting with the head of China operations for one of the world's largest media companies. He looked like a kid, and he practically is one. When you're lucky enough to catch an economic wave—as I and thousands of others were with the Internet, for example—professional life happens quick. This executive had first encountered China in college only a decade ago, when he spent a semester in Nanjing. Seeking to bolster his business-school application, he had worked at a consulting firm in Hong Kong and then at a Chinese software company founded by two Americans. The company planned to dominate the mobile-phone infrastructure business, but, on a lark, it also launched an embryonic messaging application. This sideline took over, the company went public, and the executive no longer had any need for business school. So, he took his stock options and China expertise and joined the media conglomerate, and now, in his early 30s, he is a trusted adviser to the moguls at the top.

The executive took me to a Beijing roast-duck restaurant called Hua's. In keeping with one theme of the evening, piracy, Hua's used to be one of the only restaurants on the block. Now so many places in the neighborhood have copied its formula (lanterns, lights, open-air courtyard) that we had to cruise up and down the street to find it.

Pirates Everywhere

Like other multinationals, the media conglomerate is consumed with the awesome challenge of piracy. One way to control the flood of pirated DVDs, for example, might be to trumpet the superior experience of watching movies in a theater. But Chinese movie distribution is so tightly controlled that most movies never hit the big screen. Another solution might be to cut DVD prices by 90 percent, but, at this price—for legal vendors—all profit is then taxed away. One major movie company, TimeWarner, is supposedly going this route—

selling movies for about $3 each—but the verdict is still out on whether this will succeed.

This media executive focuses primarily on interactive applications, such as online and cellphone messaging, so our conversation soon veered in that direction. But at meetings and meals in Beijing over the next few days, the piracy issue came up again and again and again.

In China, piracy is so entrenched that even the pirates complain about it. According to an article by Anne Stevenson-Yang and Ken DeWoskin in the March issue of the *Far Eastern Economic Review* [*FEER*], Chinese storekeepers who sell fake DVDs for 10 yuan gripe about street vendors selling them for seven. And the street vendors complain about competitors offering two-for-one specials.

But it's not just DVDs that are being ripped off, of course. It's *everything*. According to some estimates, as much as a third of China's GDP[1] comes from piracy and counterfeiting, including more than 90 percent of the country's software and 95 percent of its video games. In *The Chinese Century*, Oded Shenkar says that five of six of the "Yamaha" motorcycles in China are fake—in part, perhaps, because Yamaha's parts suppliers sell real Yamaha parts to fake-Yamaha assemblers. The same goes for more than half of China's razor blades, cell phones, drugs, chewing gum, and shampoo. Fast-food uniforms and business processes are copied. Electronic chips are reverse-engineered and modified to allow third parties to write add-ons, creating fake chip value chains. Fake car parts are unwittingly built into real cars—exposing the real manufacturers to liability—and real parts are built into fake products in other industries. Some fakes are crappy: movies with scratchy sound and heads visible at the bottom of the screen. Some are so good that even the manufacturers can't tell the difference. (When "North Face" jackets appear in the Xian-

---

1. Gross domestic product (GDP) is a measure of all goods and services produced in a country.

Microsoft Combats Piracy

In [Microsoft's] anti-piracy action, we have a global system and strategies, including 3 core parts, called 3E: education, engineering and enforcement. In education, we try our best to tell the customers, consumers, business partners, government, and media the risks caused by counterfeits and the advantages of legal software. We believe that it is quite important to improve people's consciousness of IPR [intellectual property rights] protection. In engineering, we spend enormous money and time to improve anti-piracy and anti-counterfeit skills, in order to avoid hacker attacks and counterfeits. In enforcement, we cooperate with many countries' governmental law enforcement agencies and related agencies, such as customs, to help them conduct IPR law enforcement in a proper, concrete, and appropriate way. . . . In the 3E strategies, education plays a key role and the other two are subsidiary.

Harry Yang, October 2008. www.chinaipmagazine.com.

gyang Park market, they aren't *like* North Face, they *are* North Face.) The new frontier, meanwhile, is export. Some estimate that 7 percent of global trade is now bogus stuff.

China Does Not Want Change

Piracy apologists, who occasionally include the Chinese government, often point out that developing countries have a long tradition of such behavior, starting with the U.S. (Charles Dickens was reportedly stiffed for royalties by U.S. publishers). In this view, the U.S. companies are hypocrites: Now that we've stolen IP, polluted the environment, and exploited workers to move up the value chain, we want to ban the practices in other countries (an argument that has some truth to it). The U.S. didn't get really tough on intellectual-property rights, people note, until we had intellectual property to lose, and the common wisdom is that the same will hold true for China. In *FEER*, however, Stevenson-Yang and DeWoskin suggest that China's situation might not follow this path to legitimacy, in part because the government has so much to gain from the status quo. Shenkar concurs: Whatever form the solution takes, it won't come anytime soon.

So, what are multinationals to do? Here are some of Stevenson-Yang, DeWoskin, and Shenkar's ideas. First, recognize that the value (or at least life span) of intellectual property may be less in the future than it has been in the past. Then, depending on the unique circumstances of each place and industry, fight like hell.

Crank up the litigators, making it painful to pirates to fake your products and thus encouraging them to rip off someone else. Redesign business processes to make it more difficult to steal stuff, and consider what you do lose a cost of doing business. Pay for your own enforcement raids. Don't do China joint-ventures, which function as a siphon tube through which local entrepreneurs suck out ideas, technology, and products. Design your products to have shorter life cycles, thus leaving pirates stuck with warehouses full of outdated stuff. Cut prices, making piracy less profitable. Give away technology in hopes of establishing a standard that you can control. Offer local pricing: Don't force people who make $1,000 a year to pay $250 for an office suite. Shift to a service/support model, and give your products away for free.

One of the most intractable elements of the problem, of course—one that all companies are eventually forced to acknowledge—is that products are not worth what the manufacturers say they are worth but what customers are willing to pay for them. The reason pirated products are so wildly popular is that customers *love* their value proposition. Even the greatest minds in the antipiracy business can't wait to snag $1 copies of first-run movies and $10 copies of Windows XP—products that, they rightly observe, often play or run as well as versions that cost 20 times as much. With digital products, at least, China's piracy epidemic may prove to be the great profit-margin equalizer. No longer, perhaps, will companies like Microsoft be able to earn 80 percent profit margins—because, sick of feeling gouged, customers are nothing less than thrilled to help rip the companies off.

Periodical Bibliography

The following articles have been selected to supplement the diverse views presented in this chapter.

Andrew Batson — "China Rises on Power of Stimulus," *Wall Street Journal*, July 16, 2009. http://online.wsj.com.

Economist — "Battle of Ideas," April 23, 2009. www.economist.com.

Economist — "China's Recovery: A Fine Balancing Act," July 16, 2009. www.economist.com.

Economist — "A Time for Muscle-Flexing," March 21, 2009. www.economist.com.

James Fallows — "China's Way Forward," *Atlantic*, April 2009. www.theatlantic.com.

Edwar Prasad — "The U.S. and China: A Grand Bargain?" Brookings Institution, July 23, 2009. www.brookings.edu.

Irwin Stelzer — "China Profits from Open Markets but Curbs Free Trade," *Times* (London), July 18, 2009. http://business.timesonline.co.uk.

Wieland Wagner — "As Orders Dry Up, Factory Workers Head Home," *Der Spiegel* (Hamburg, Germany), January 8, 2009, trans. Christopher Sultan. www.spiegel.de.

Rupert Walker — "China's Free-Trade Credentials Under the Spotlight," *BusinessWeek*, July 22, 2009. www.businessweek.com.

J.R. Wu — "China Overtakes Germany in GDP, Becomes Third-Largest Economy," *Wall Street Journal*, January 15, 2009. http://online.wsj.com.

OPPOSING
VIEWPOINTS®
SERIES

CHAPTER 3

Is China's Military a Threat?

Chapter Preface

China's economic expansion has allowed it to invest heavily in increased military capability. This has caused concern in the United States and elsewhere. However, the expansion of military power has also made it possible for China to make significant contributions to peacekeeping forces. As recently as 2000, China has contributed fewer than a hundred personnel to United Nations peacekeeping operations. By 2007, that number had risen to eighteen hundred troops, observers, and police.

There are several reasons for China to contribute more to peacekeeping forces worldwide. First, Chin-Hao Hung and Bates Gill note in a 2009 article on the ISN Web site, "Positive engagement with the outside world helps China project a more benign . . . image beyond its borders." In addition, troops deployed as peacekeepers gain useful practical experience and improve their readiness for riot control, coordination, and military operations.

In addition, according to an article on the Stratfor Web site published in 2007, joining UN missions can help China secure its own interests abroad. China has increasing investments overseas and requires more and more energy for its expanding economy. Sending troops to stabilize China's trading partner Sudan, for example, Stratfor argues, would raise U.S. objections. "Operating as part of a UN mission, however," Stratfor notes, "lends China's expansion into international security operations a more peace-oriented, nonthreatening cast; it gives the impression that China is spending its security budget overseas not just for itself, but for the world."

China's decision to become more involved in peacekeeping has, then, met with mixed responses. On the one hand, China has contributed naval vessels to help defend against piracy off the coast of Somalia. In doing so, it has worked closely with the United States, the North Atlantic Treaty Organization (NATO) states, and Europe, and it has been almost universally acclaimed for doing so. On the other hand, however, China's growing ability to send troops great distances, and its interests in places like Africa, have been a cause for some concern. J. Peter Pham, for example, argued in a 2007 column for *World Defense Review* that Chinese "'peacekeeping' between Ethiopia and Eritrea ... is not without its ironies ... as both governments are armed to the teeth thanks, in no small part, to the estimated $1 billion in arms sold to both of them by the PRC [People's Republic of China]."

Ultimately, as this discussion demonstrates, China's growing military power has created opportunities and challenges not only for China but for the United States and the rest of the world. The following viewpoints examine other ways in which Chinese military strength has affected world security, for better or worse.

> *"China has become one of the Pentagon's most pressing concerns, ranking just below Iraq, terrorism, and Iran."*

China's Military Buildup Is a Threat to U.S. Interests

John J. Tkacik Jr.

John J. Tkacik Jr. is a retired diplomat who is now a senior research fellow in Asian Studies at the Heritage Foundation, a conservative think tank in Washington, D.C. In the following viewpoint, Tkacik argues that because of its military buildup, China has become a major source of concern for the U.S. military. Tkacik contends that China's expanded nuclear capability threatens the U.S. directly, its expanded conventional forces threaten allies in Taiwan and Japan, and its ambitions threaten the entire East Asia region and beyond. Tkacik argues that the U.S. needs to develop plans to contain the danger from China.

As you read, consider the following questions:

1. Tkacik notes that what Chinese weapons are capable of striking targets in the United States?

John J. Tkacik Jr., "Panda Hedging: Pentagon Report Urges New Strategy for China," Heritage Foundation Web Memo #1093, May 24, 2006. Copyright © 2006 The Heritage Foundation. Reproduced by permission.

2. According to the author, how many short-range ballistic missiles may China have trained on Taiwan as of April 2006?

3. According to General Liu, as quoted by Tkacik, why should China improve relations with Muslim countries?

The Pentagon's fifth annual "Report on the Military Power of the People's Republic of China" was sent to Congress this week [in May 2006]. Even more than its predecessors, this year's report is unsettling, with myriad disturbing revelations: the military balance across the Taiwan Strait[1] has now tipped in China's favor; China's military doctrine appears to view Taiwan as a stepping stone to a broader and farther reaching strategic presence in the Western Pacific; China's military has made major advances in strategic weapons; the Chinese military is in the midst of a debate on a new, more threatening nuclear doctrine; and China is far from behaving as a responsible stakeholder in the global community. As the new report confirms, "hedging" has become the watchword in China relations in Washington. It's about time.

China Threatens the U.S. Directly

Over the past year, China has become one of the Pentagon's most pressing concerns, ranking just below Iraq, terrorism, and Iran. In February [2006] the Pentagon's Quadrennial Defense Review (QDR), a strategic planning document issued every four years, warned that "the pace and scope of China's military build-up already puts regional military balances at risk." The QDR, for the first time, named China as a potential military competitor. While the QDR allowed that "U.S. policy remains focused on encouraging China to play a constructive, peaceful role in the Asia-Pacific region," the Pentagon also seeks to create "prudent hedges against the possibility that cooperative approaches by themselves may fail to preclude fu-

---

1. Taiwan is a self-governing island technically claimed by Communist China.

ture conflict." In March, President [George W.] Bush's "National Security Strategy" also described a public policy to "encourage China to make the right strategic decisions for its people while we hedge against other possibilities." [The] Pentagon report asserts that "China's military expansion is already such as to alter regional military balances." The Pentagon now believes that "international reactions to China's military growth will understandably provide resistance against" the unknowns of China's nontransparent strategic goals. While the Administration still seeks "cooperation" with China, "hedging" China is now the other side of the policy coin.

China's sudden military rise is not a figment of the White House's imagination. Last fall [2005], Dr. Kurt Campbell, Deputy Assistant Secretary of Defense for Asian and Pacific Affairs during the [Bill] Clinton Administration, professed his astonishment at China's incredibly rapid military modernization. "You look back on those [intelligence] studies, and it's only been a decade," he marveled. "China has exceeded—in every area of military modernization—that which even the far-off estimates of the mid-1990s predicted." Indeed, in [the] report, the Pentagon admits that "several aspects of China's military development have surprised U.S. analysts, including the pace and scope of its strategic forces modernization."

China's rapid strategic forces modernization is the biggest threat. The People's Liberation Army's (PLA)[2] intense focus on "power-projection" and "area denial" capabilities is well into its tenth year. China's military now boasts our new ICBMs[3] poised for imminent deployment. The Dongfeng-31 ICBM will be ready [in 2006], and its advanced sibling, the DF-31A, will be on the launch pad [in 2007]. The Julang-1 and 2 submarine-launched ICBMs should be ready for the new "JIN" (type 094) class nuclear submarine by 2010. All are

2. The PLA is China's military.
3. An ICBM, or intercontinental ballistic missile, is a long-range missile designed to carry nuclear weapons.

capable of striking targets in the continental United States. These missile advances come at the same time as an unprecedented Chinese naval procurement program, which has at least five new classes of submarine under development simultaneously.

The Pentagon's concerns are sharpened by indications that the PLA is debating "the value of China's 'no first use' nuclear policy." Last July [2005], a delegation of foreign media editors based in Hong Kong visited Beijing, where they were treated to a disquisition on nuclear war theory by PLA general Zhu Chenghu. Page 28 of the Pentagon report cites General Zhu's words: "[I]f the Americans draw their missiles and position guided ammunition [sic] onto the target zone on China's territory, I think we will have to respond with nuclear weapons." The report also quotes another Chinese strategist, Chu Shulong, as cautioning that "China may renounce this commitment [to no first use] at a time when the country's fate hangs in the balance." Another Chinese scholar of nuclear doctrine, Shen Dingli, opined that "if China's conventional forces are devastated . . . it is inconceivable that China would allow its nuclear weapons to be destroyed by a precision attack with conventional munitions, rather than use them as a true means of deterrence." Such statements (along with similar views expressed by other PLA officers directly to visiting U.S. military officers) lead the Pentagon to consider how it might influence the "terms of this debate or affect Beijing's thinking about its nuclear options in the future."

China Threatens Taiwan and Japan

Among the other key developments enumerated in the report's first chapter is the judgment that "China's expansion of missile and other military forces opposite Taiwan has continued unabated with the balance of forces shifting in the mainland's favor." In other words, the balance has already shifted, just as promised in earlier assessments, which calculated that 2005

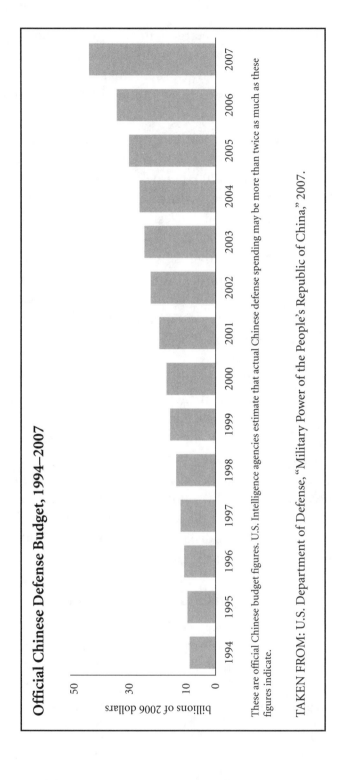

Official Chinese Defense Budget, 1994–2007

billions of 2006 dollars

1994 1995 1996 1997 1998 1999 2000 2001 2002 2003 2004 2005 2006 2007

50 30 10 0

These are official Chinese budget figures. U.S. Intelligence agencies estimate that actual Chinese defense spending may be more than twice as much as these figures indicate.

TAKEN FROM: U.S. Department of Defense, "Military Power of the People's Republic of China," 2007.

would be the tipping point for Taiwan—especially if its own military stagnated. The new report estimates that China has 710 to 790 short-range ballistic missiles [SRBMs] trained on Taiwan "as of late 2005." In fact, administration sources confirm privately that the Pentagon puts the number at 810 SRBMs, as of April 2006.

All this presents a major challenge to the Defense Department, which is congressionally mandated by the Taiwan Relations Act . . . "to maintain the capacity of the United States to resist any resort to force or other forms of coercion" against Taiwan—a mandate the report explicitly cites. The report asserts that China should be deterred from aggression against Taiwan by "the virtual certainty of U.S. intervention, and Japanese interests" and should view "the United States, especially in combination with Japan," as having the upper hand in "many scenarios involving the use of force"—for now, at least.

But Taiwan is just one of the Pentagon's concerns. The report also cites instances of provocative moves by the Chinese military against Japan, including the incursion of a Chinese nuclear submarine into Japanese territorial waters near Okinawa and a well-publicized incident in September 2005 in which "PLA Navy vessels trained their weapons on Japanese aircraft monitoring Chinese drilling" in Japanese-claimed waters in the East China Sea. The report leaves unmentioned other similar incidents. These incidents lead many in the Bush Administration to wonder if the Chinese navy is intentionally irritating the Japanese to see if the United States will support its main strategic ally in East Asia.

China Hegemony

Aside from episodes of Chinese aggressiveness towards Taiwan and Japan, the Pentagon report notes several instances of pointedly unhelpful behavior from China. China has a "unique potential" to pressure North Korea on its nuclear ambitions but doesn't; it did, however, pressure its Central Asian allies to "call for a date for the withdrawal of U.S. forces prosecuting the War on Terrorism in Central Asia." It promoted Asian "regional institutions that would exclude the United States" such as the East Asia Summit and the ASEAN+3 dialogue.[4] China has dubious "political links with states such as Iran, Sudan, Burma, Zimbabwe, Cuba and Venezuela." Further, "Chinese companies continue to play a negative role" in nuclear and missile proliferation. And perhaps most recklessly, China continues "to supply countries like Iran with critical military technologies."

As it did last year [in 2005], the Pentagon report notes that "Beijing is also surveying the strategic landscape beyond Taiwan." This year, the report cites Chinese General Liu Yazhou's matter-of-fact observation that "when a nation grows strong enough, it practices hegemony." General Liu was talking about China, not the United States. General Liu, son-in-law of late Chinese president Li Xiannian, speaks like a true Chinese "princeling": "Geography is destiny . . . when a country begins to rise, it should first set itself in an invincible position." What the Pentagon report doesn't cite are General Liu's assertions from last year that China's improved relations with Muslim countries were "an excellent move" because China "should do what the West fears."

With the word "hedging" featuring conspicuously in February's QDR, March's White House National Security Strategy, and now the Pentagon's China Report, it is clear that "hedging" is now the watchword of U.S. China policy. A "hedging" strategy with China is exactly what is needed in Washington now. For the sake of U.S. national security, that word, and the ideas and observations it embodies, must develop into a coherent policy set.

---

4. The East Asia Summit is an annual forum of leaders of sixteen countries in East Asia. ASEAN+3 is a summit of Southeast Asian nations plus China, Japan, and South Korea.

> "Beijing's armed forces remain dwarfed
> by America's military, which starts at a
> vastly higher base and spends several
> times as much."

China's Military Buildup Is Not a Threat to Legitimate U.S. Interests

Doug Bandow

Doug Bandow is a senior fellow at the Cato Institute and the author of Foreign Follies: America's New Global Empire. *In this viewpoint, he argues that China does not have the capability to attack or threaten the United States. Instead, China's military buildup, he insists, is defensive, designed to protect the Chinese mainland from American attack. Bandow argues that American vital interests do not require U.S. dominance in Asia, and that therefore the Chinese buildup should not be a cause for concern.*

As you read, consider the following questions:

1. According to Bandow, how many nuclear missiles does China have?

2. What is China's military buildup focused on, in the author' opinion?

Doug Bandow, "China's Military Rise Means End of U.S. Hegemony?" *Korea Times*, May 5, 2009, Opinion. Reproduced by permission of the author.

3. According to Bandow, which American interests are vital?

U. S. military spending continues to increase even though conventional threats against the United States are de minimis [minimal]. China is the leading contender for Enemy Number 1.

But if Beijing poses a threat, it is to U.S. domination of East Asia, not the country itself. Only the latter is worth fighting for. Commonly expressed is fear of growing Chinese military outlays.

China Is No Challenge

The Pentagon highlighted its concern with the latest annual report on the Chinese defense budget. Yet Beijing's armed forces remain dwarfed by America's military, which starts at a vastly higher base and spends several times as much.

The Pentagon report states that the United States "encourages China to participate responsibly in the international system." True enough, but how does Washington define "responsibly"?

One suspects it means accepting American military hegemony in East Asia—something with which Beijing isn't likely to agree.

The Chinese military buildup so far has been significant but measured. "The People's Liberation Army (PLA) is pursuing comprehensive transformation from a mass army designed for protracted wars of attrition on its periphery against high-tech adversaries," explains the Pentagon.

Moreover, China's "armed forces continue to develop and field disruptive military technologies, including those for anti-access/area-denial, as well as for nuclear, space, and cyber warfare, that are changing regional military balances and that have implications beyond the Asia-Pacific region."

Yet this concerted expansion little threatens U.S. security. Only the Chinese nuclear force is theoretically able to strike America today. Beijing possesses about 60 missiles, some of limited range.

In contrast, the U.S. nuclear arsenal includes thousands of sophisticated warheads on hundreds of missiles. Beijing is going to have to spend years to build a modest force simply capable of deterring America.

Of course, China intends to move beyond its own shores. China is "developing longer-range capabilities that have implications beyond Taiwan,"[1] which "could allow China to project power to ensure access to resources or enforce claims to disputed territories," warns the Pentagon.

However, notes the Department of Defense (DOD), China's military "continues to face deficiencies in inter-service cooperation and actual experience in joint exercises and combat operations." Moreover, Beijing is not yet capable of "defeating a moderate-size adversary."

The Pentagon adds, "China will not be able to project and sustain small military units far beyond China before 2015, and will not be able to project and sustain large forces in combat operations far from China until well into the following decade."

In any case, China has minimal strategic conventional reach. The United States possesses 11 carrier groups to China's none. Beijing also lacks a significant strategic air capability.

East Asian countries may be at greater risk, but defending these nations—which are largely capable of protecting themselves—is not the same as defending the United States.

China's most obvious objective is to create a military capable of enforcing its will on Taiwan. However, tensions in the Taiwan Strait have eased and the DOD admits that "an attempt to invade Taiwan would strain China's untested armed

1. A self-governing island claimed by China.

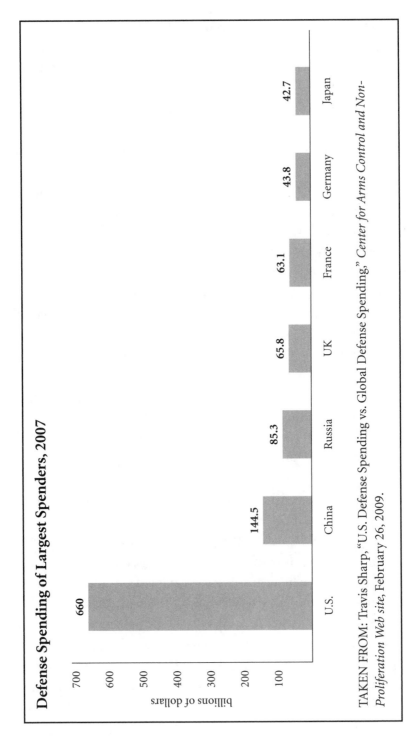

Defense Spending of Largest Spenders, 2007

billions of dollars

U.S.	660
China	144.5
Russia	85.3
UK	65.8
France	63.1
Germany	43.8
Japan	42.7

TAKEN FROM: Travis Sharp, "U.S. Defense Spending vs. Global Defense Spending," *Center for Arms Control and Non-Proliferation Web site*, February 26, 2009.

forces and invite international intervention." Taipei [Taiwan's largest city] also could do significantly more to protect itself.

Deterring the United States

In fact, Beijing's military buildup is focused on preventing the United States from attacking China. The Pentagon admits as much without explicitly saying that Beijing is focused on deterring Washington.

China has or is acquiring the ability to:

1. Hold large surface ships—including aircraft carriers—at risk (via quiet submarines, advanced anti-ship cruise missiles (ASCMs), wire-guided and wake-homing torpedoes, or anti-ship ballistic missiles)

2. Deny the use of shore-based airfields, secure bastions and regional logistics hubs (via conventional ballistic missiles with greater ranges and accuracy, and land attack cruise missiles)

3. Hold aircraft at risk over or near Chinese territory or forces (via imported and domestic fourth generation aircraft, advanced long-range surface-to-air missile systems, air surveillance systems and ship-borne air defense)

Who would be sending in "large surface ships" using "shore-based airfields, secure bastions and regional logistics hubs," and deploying aircraft against China—Don't ask.

Washington has vital interests to protect, but not all of its interests are vital. Defending American territory, liberties, and people at home is vital; ensuring dominant American influence half a world away is not.

And doing the latter at acceptable cost will grow ever more difficult. By spending a fraction of the United States' defense budget, Beijing is constructing a military able to deter U.S. intervention against China.

To overcome this force Washington will have to spend far more—money which it does not have.

With China on the move, the DOD observes that "the United States continues to work with our allies and friends in the region to monitor these developments and adjust our policies accordingly."

But the resulting policy adjustment should be reducing U.S. international ambitions rather than increasing military spending. Washington should replace dominance with defense as the core of its foreign policy.

*"The United States and China should
be the strongest advocates for reducing
the currency of nuclear weapons."*

China Can Aid Nuclear Nonproliferation

Xiaohui Anne Wu

*Xiaohui Anne Wu is an associate of the Managing the Atom
Project at the Belfer Center for Science and International Affairs
at Harvard University's Kennedy School of Government. In the
following viewpoint, she argues that the United States and China
have a common interest in reducing nuclear proliferation. Wu
suggests that the United States could advance nonproliferation by
recognizing China's concerns about U.S. willingness to launch a
preemptive nuclear strike and about U.S. support for India's
nuclear weapons program. In return, China could be a major
ally in dealing with the nuclear issue in North Korea, Iran, and
other areas, Wu contends.*

As you read, consider the following questions:

1. Internationally, China and the United States are committed to promoting nonproliferation within the framework of what institutions, according to Wu?

2. According to the author, does China claim the right to preemptively use its nuclear weapons?

3. According to Wu, why do many Chinese believe it is unfair for the United States to ask other countries not to develop nuclear weapons?

The position of [then Democratic presidential candidate] Barack Obama and [then Republican presidential candidate] John McCain on the [George W.] Bush administration's latest deal with North Korea indicate different approaches that each might take on non-proliferation issues—engagement or containment. While both consider nuclear nonproliferation a priority and both endorse the idea that the United States should take serious steps toward eliminating nuclear weapons, the North Korean issue highlights the importance for the United States to engage one of its most important partners for accomplishing these goals—China.

North Korea and Beyond

China's crucial role has not been diminished since the North Korean denuclearization process started in 2003, even if the United States later started direct dialogue with Pyongyang [the North Korean capital]. Indeed, it was just reported that Washington expects Pyongyang to submit to China a list of verification steps it would allow in return for being removed from the U.S. terrorism-sponsor list.

Yet the North Korean issue only represents one piece of international non-proliferation efforts. At a time when the global non-proliferation regime is weakened in the absence of consensus on priority and process, China and the U.S. share a common interest and responsibility to strengthen measures that prevent the proliferation of nuclear weapons. The two countries both agree and disagree on nuclear non-proliferation.

Internationally, the two countries are committed to promoting non-proliferation within frameworks such as the United Nations, the International Atomic Energy Agency (IAEA) and the Nuclear Suppliers Group (NSG).

Regionally, they maintain consultations on the nuclear issue on the Korean Peninsula and in Iran. Bilaterally, they have intensified dialogues and cooperation on export control and intelligence sharing, as well as in other areas. Yet differences, ranging from strategic to practical issues, remain. The ... president, together with the Chinese leadership, must lead by example through more effective cooperation. The United States and China should be the strongest advocates for reducing the currency of nuclear weapons.

How to Cooperate

One thing in the way of their partnership is their differing views on their own nuclear weapons. Since going nuclear in 1964, China has been committed to a policy of no-first-use of nuclear weapons and no use of nuclear weapons against non-nuclear states or in nuclear-free zones. The United States, on the other hand, reserves its right, as part of its nuclear doctrine, to strike others in a pre-emptive manner.

Many Chinese believe that it is unfair for the U.S. to ask other countries to not develop nuclear weapons while it maintains a huge nuclear stockpile. And its policies are counterproductive because they continue to provide legitimacy to nuclear weapons in international affairs. The United States and China must bridge their respective perceptions of potential nuclear threat and approaches to non-proliferation in order to work together to tackle the most urgent nuclear problems.

The United States could engage China more effectively on concerns, such as the North Korean and Iranian nuclear issues, by recognizing China's own interests. Denuclearization efforts will not succeed without China's support, and the perception that the United States is only using China's influence

India and Nonproliferation

President [George W.] Bush agreed to give India virtual membership in the club of recognized nuclear-weapons states created by the Nuclear Nonproliferation Treaty.

The NPT dates back to 1968, when five states had tested nuclear weapons: Britain, China, France, Russia . . . and the US. The treaty was a deal between them and the rest of the world; the "haves" would, over time, negotiate the reduction and eventual elimination of their nuclear arsenals (the latter goal was a blue-sky dream that has never been seriously pursued), and the "have-nots" would refrain from acquiring nukes in exchange for . . . assistance in developing peaceful uses of nuclear energy.

By conducting an underground test that caught the world by surprise in May 1998, India put itself unambiguously and irreversibly outside the bounds of the treaty.

Strobe Talbott, Yale Global, *July 21, 2005.*

to reduce a nuclear threat to itself is detrimental to bilateral relations. Regarding North Korea and Iran, China envisions nuclear non-proliferation as a broad security concept that encompasses all-around solutions. China believes that the fundamental purpose of non-proliferation is to safeguard and promote regional and international peace and security. To achieve these goals, non-proliferation should be pursued in a diplomatic manner that eschews coercion and other hostile measures.

China also advocates equilibrium between non-proliferation, peaceful uses of nuclear energy, and disarmament. Because of its perceived balanced stance on North Korea and Iran, China occupies the formidable middle ground and could play a constructive role in facilitating a solution that avoids full-scale crisis. The United States should encourage China to continue its constructive intervention: no nuclear-weapons program, no escalating confrontations, but continued, flexible dialogue. Otherwise, should any of the parties up the ante, the international community will lose a valuable avenue to mitigate the crisis.

The United States can facilitate China's efforts on regional arms control and security by maintaining consistent standards. Supporting nuclear trade with India, which stands outside of the nuclear non-proliferation treaty, blurs those standards.

In a rare public response to the controversial U.S. proposal to lift a ban on nuclear trade with India, the *People's Daily*, China's largest official newspaper, carried an editorial saying: "Whether it is motivated by geopolitical considerations or commercial interests, the U.S.-India nuclear agreement has constituted a major blow to the international non-proliferation regime."

The United States should recognize China's solid position in defending the global non-proliferation regime, and its active role in reducing regional proliferation tensions. The U.S. should support, with China, a more constructive means of countering nuclear proliferation, both regionally and internationally. As Albert Einstein said, "Every kind of peaceful cooperation among men is primarily based on mutual trust and only secondly on institutions." The . . . U.S. president must work to deepen mutual trust in Sino-U.S. relations for the benefit of both parties and the world.

| "North Korea is a puppet state, and the Chinese are the puppeteers."

China Is Behind the North Korean Threat

Anne Applebaum

Anne Applebaum is a Pulitzer Prize–winning author and a weekly columnist for the Washington Post. *In the following viewpoint, she argues that China controls North Korea's government and its policies. Therefore, she says, North Korean nuclear tests, and its other belligerent actions, are part of deliberate Chinese policy. Applebaum suggests that China is using North Korea to test American resolve without endangering U.S.-Chinese relations.*

As you read, consider the following questions:

1. According to Applebaum, what could China do to topple North Korea's government?

2. As described by the author, when did China say it learned of North Korean plans for a recent nuclear test?

3. According to Applebaum, China may be looking to distract and disturb the new Obama administration without suffering what consequences?

Anne Applebaum, "Shadow Boxing in Pyongyang," *Washington Post*, June 2, 2009, Opinion. Reproduced by permission of the author.

Cutting Oil to North Korea

China cut off oil exports to North Korea in September [2006], amid heightened tensions over that country's nuclear and missile programs, Chinese trade statistics show.

The unusual move—the figures show China sold no crude oil at all to its neighbor in September—reduced cumulative sales for the year by about 7 percent over the same period in 2005. China's oil exports to Pyongyang had been averaging about 50,000 metric tons a month this year.

Joseph Kahn,
New York Times, *October 30, 2006.*

Let's face it: We don't really know why North Korea decided to test a nuclear weapon last week [in May 2009], why it has suddenly declared the Korean War armistice of 1953 null and void, why it has launched several test missiles and is preparing to launch others. It could be because the North Koreans are dissatisfied with the state of negotiations with Washington and want more concessions or more attention. It could be that the regime—which is no longer capable of delivering regular food supplies, or even reliable electricity, to its people—wanted to strengthen its grip on power. It could be something else altogether. Personally, I favor another scenario, equally speculative: Perhaps the North Koreans have stepped up their war rhetoric, and their war preparations, because China wants them to do so. I cannot prove that this is the case—just as no one else can prove any of their theories about North Korea—but I can look at the evidence, which is as follows:

Means and Motive

China is the one country that actually has influence over North Korea. Not only is China the only country to maintain frequent diplomatic and security contacts with North Korea, but China could, if it wanted to, topple the North Korean regime tomorrow. China could cut off North Korea's oil. China could shut the border to trade. Or China could take the opposite tactic and open the border: Refugees would flee and the regime would crumble, much as East Germany did 20 years ago. To put it differently, China has more influence over the North Korean regime than all of the other U.N. Security Council members put together, but it does not use this influence to stop Pyongyang's [North Korea's capital] nuclear program. Instead, it has maintained trade relations, kept the oil flowing, built up its border fences and paid lip service to the international efforts to block the North Korean nuclear program (the Chinese claimed to have learned about the recent nuclear test an hour in advance, which no one believes), all while hunkering down to watch what happens.

China has ambitions to replace the United States as the dominant power in East Asia. For proof, look no further than the money the Chinese have spent lately on expanding their navy, which now includes at least 70 submarines, 10 of which are thought to be nuclear. By contrast, the United States has between 70 and 80 submarines deployed at any given moment, but they patrol the whole world, not just Asian waters. The Chinese are also now designing aircraft carriers and reportedly now have long-range, anti-ship ballistic missiles—the better to destroy our aircraft carriers—as well.

Testing America

China knows the rest of Asia is watching this test of the [Barack] Obama administration. And if, as seems likely, the Obama administration does not come up with a way to stop North

Korea's nuclear program, what conclusions will the South Koreans draw—not to mention the Japanese? Or the Taiwanese? Might some of them not conclude that the American security umbrella no longer seems quite as wide and strong as it used to? Might they not conclude that they are better off under Chinese protection? This would, of course, be a somewhat far-fetched and risky game, if the Chinese were indeed playing it: After all, the Japanese are not known to be enthusiastic about the prospect of Chinese domination, and the Taiwanese are not known to be interested in reunification with the mainland.[1] Rather than falling in line, the Japanese might instead conclude that they need their own nuclear deterrent. The South Koreans might follow, the Taiwanese might add to their own mighty naval fleet, and then a deadly Asian arms race would be underway.

Despite the risks, though, there are good reasons for the Chinese to prod [North Korean leader] Kim Jong Il to keep those missiles coming. By permitting North Korea to rattle its sabers, the Chinese can monitor President Obama's reaction to a military threat—without having to deploy a threat themselves. They can see how serious the new American administration is about controlling the spread of nuclear weapons—without having to risk sanctions or international condemnation of their own nuclear industry. They can distract and disturb the new administration—without harming Chinese American economic relations, which are crucial to their own regime's stability. And if the game goes badly, they can call it off altogether. North Korea is a puppet state, and the Chinese are the puppeteers. They could end this farce tomorrow. If they haven't done so yet, there must be a reason.

1. Taiwan is a self-governing island; it was once part of, and is still claimed by, China.

> "It is time for the United States and
> China to act jointly to free the Korean
> peninsula from its cold war shackles
> and address the underlying causes of
> the North Korean nuclear crisis."

China Can Help Confront the North Korean Threat

Martin Malin and Hui Zhang

*Martin Malin is executive director and Hui Zhang is a research
associate at the Project on Managing the Atom in the Belfer
Center for Science and International Affairs at Harvard's
Kennedy School of Government. In the following viewpoint, they
argue that both the United States and China have an interest in
forcing North Korea to renounce nuclear weapons and in stabi-
lizing the region. The authors say that China and the United
States can and should work together to end the North Korean
crisis.*

As you read, consider the following questions:

1. According to the authors, how did China bring North
   Korea to the negotiating table in 2003?

Martin Malin and Hui Zhang, "US and China Must Stand Up to N. Korea," *Boston
Globe*, May 31, 2009, Op-Ed. Reproduced by permission of the authors.

2. China is worried that the Korean crisis will provide a pretext for accelerating the deployment of what, according to Malin and Zhang?

3. Does the United States intend to move troops to the Chinese border in case of a North Korean collapse, according to the authors?

Shockwaves continue to emanate from the Korea peninsula following North Korea's recent [2009] nuclear and missile tests. Time is not on the side of those who want to put an end to the dangers posed by North Korea. The longer the crisis lasts, the more nuclear-capable North Korea will become; the risk of confrontation will increase, as will the price of getting North Korea to step back from the brink. The key to moving beyond the current impasse is coordinated action by the United States and China in the Security Council and beyond.

The Six Party Talks

Washington holds what Pyongyang [the North Korean capital] most wants and China has the most direct leverage on North Korea.

North Korea wants direct engagement with Washington toward a normalization of relations. Even as the Security Council deliberates on a new round of sanctions, in exchange for refreezing all plutonium production, Washington must offer North Korea the promise of immediate talks under the Six Party framework[1] on ending the state of war.[2] This symbolic step would provide significant reassurance to Pyongyang as the North Korean regime contends with a leadership transition.

---

1. The Six Party talks are diplomatic negotiations among China, Russia, South Korea, Japan, the United States, and North Korea dedicated to resolving security concerns about North Korea's nuclear weapons program.
2. The Korean War never officially ended, so North and South Korea are still technically in a state of war.

The next step should be a return to the process of disabling and then dismantling North Korea's nuclear facilities, as agreed previously. A new roadmap that links North Korean denuclearization with the gradual delivery of concrete benefits, based on the "action for action" principle, would facilitate subsequent steps. Destinations on this roadmap should include security assurances, full diplomatic normalization, economic reform, and Northeast Asian security cooperation. The United States must take the first step.

Beijing must press Pyongyang to accept Washington's offer. As North Korea's ally for more than 50 years, China has the most direct means of exerting influence. North Korea depends on China for up to 90 percent of its oil and for much of its food aid.

Beijing must support new Security Council sanctions and begin tying the supply of oil and food aid to Pyongyang's cooperation. Such an approach promises to bring results: In 2003, Beijing temporarily shut down an oil pipeline to North Korea for "technical reasons" and reportedly played a key role in bringing the North Koreans to the negotiating table.

China should make clear that North Korea cannot have both nuclear weapons and an end to its isolation. A continuing crisis will only generate increasing international pressure and economic sanctions, further devastating the already suffering North Korean economy.

Both Want the Crisis Ended

China and the United States both have critical interests in resolving the North Korean crisis. For the United States, the danger of North Korea secretly transferring nuclear materials or technology to another state (as it reportedly did with Syria) or to a terrorist group is the most serious concern.

Additional North Korean nuclear and missile tests could also expand Pyongyang's nuclear-strike capability beyond South Korea and Japan to US territory. North Korean intran-

North Korea Breaks Armistice

North Korea has declared [on May 27, 2009,] it is no longer bound by the Armistice Agreement that ended the Korean War....

The North claimed that South Korea and the United States had violated the agreement through the U.S.-led Proliferation Security Initiative (PSI), which in part focuses on stopping North Korean vessels involved in the transfer of nuclear or missile technology to other states....

The North Korean military's announcement ... was coupled with threats that North Korea's military could no longer guarantee the safety of U.S. or South Korean ships or aircraft along the west coast of North Korea.

Stratfor, May 27, 2009.
www.stratfor.com.

sigence also threatens major elements of [U.S. president] Barack Obama's global nuclear security agenda, providing political fodder to critics who oppose a nuclear test ban, fissile material cutoff, and the prospect of deep reductions in US and Russian nuclear arsenals. North Korean defiance undermines nuclear nonproliferation norms just as the world prepares for a vital review conference for the Nuclear Nonproliferation Treaty.

Beijing shares these concerns and has others. Preserving stability in the region, which is indispensable to China's economic development, is Beijing's top priority. A nuclear-armed North Korea will feed the impulses of Japan, South Korea, and even Taiwan to reconsider the option of acquiring their own nuclear weapons.

China is worried that the Korean nuclear and missile crisis will provide a pretext for accelerating the deployment of a joint US-Japanese missile defense shield, which undermines China's own modest deterrent force.

China also fears a large influx of Korean refugees in the event of a worsening crisis. And terrorist groups within China, such as those in "East Turkestan" [the Uighurs] in Xingjian with links to external groups, could attempt to acquire nuclear weapons or fissile materials from North Korea.

Working Together

To facilitate enhanced Chinese support for North Korean denuclearization, Washington should also address some of Beijing's security concerns, including US-Japanese missile defense cooperation and sales of missile defense capabilities to Taiwan. The United States and China could also offer one another specific assurances regarding military deployments on the Korean peninsula. Even in the event of a North Korean collapse, the United States has no intention of moving its forces to the Chinese border; it would reduce Beijing's concerns if Washington said so.

The Six Party talks should provide a forum for negotiating a permanent peace in northeast Asia. It is time for the United States and China to act jointly to free the Korean peninsula from its cold war shackles and address the underlying causes of the North Korean nuclear crisis.

Regardless of Pyongyang's intention, if Washington and Beijing really cannot tolerate a nuclear North Korea, the United States must offer a path forward, and China must push North Korea from behind.

| "Despite the so-called 'peace' in the Taiwan Strait, China remains a bully and will not hesitate to threaten [Taiwan], even when things are going its way."

China Remains a Threat to Taiwan

J. Michael Cole

J. Michael Cole is a Canadian journalist currently working as a columnist and editor at an English-language newspaper in Taipei, Taiwan. In the following viewpoint, he argues that China continues to threaten and bully Taiwan. As evidence, he points to Chinese missiles still pointed at Taiwan and to the words of Chinese officials. Cole argues that, contrary to the position of current Taiwanese president Ma Ying-jeou, Taiwan should expose China's bullying and push for complete independence.

As you read, consider the following questions:

1. Where did the meeting take place between Wu Shumin and Hsiao Bi-khim, as stated by the author?

2. According to Cole, how many missiles does China continue to aim at Taiwan?

J. Michael Cole, "China Advertises Itself," *The Far-Eastern Sweet Potato*, June 13, 2009. Reproduced by permission of the author.

3. What did three DPP Taipei City Councilors do to protest against the ruling party, according to the author?

It's been a good past 30 days [May–June 2009] for Taiwanese independence.[1] First, on May 18, Department of Health Minister Yeh Ching-chuan—with media in Geneva present—was administered a strong dose of anger by Taiwanese over the government's participation at the World Health Assembly meeting under the name "Chinese Taipei."

Many Taiwanese Want Independence

Though the outburst humiliated Yeh, it also showed the world that a large proportion of Taiwanese are not satisfied with the Ma Ying-jeou administration's opaque and dangerously rushed dialogue with Beijing. With daily headlines in foreign media describing the situation in the Taiwan Strait as one of unhampered rapprochement and closer ties, people outside Taiwan could be forgiven for believing that all Taiwanese are united behind Ma, that they all support his policies on China. As I have written before, the bumps in the road—and there are many—have largely been ignored, and if it takes incidents such as Yeh's public humiliation to raise awareness about the substantial opposition that exists in Taiwan, then so be it.

Ironically, it was a Chinese official in Fukuoka, Japan, who put shoulder to the wheel of the Taiwanese independence movement, this time by showing the true nature of the Chinese Communist Party's policy on Taiwan.

The principal actors in this little scene are Chinese Consulate-General in Fukuoka Wu Shumin and Democratic Progressive Party (DPP) Department of International Affairs Director Hsiao Bi-khim, with minor roles for US Consulate

---

1. Taiwan is a self-governing island, but it is claimed by China. Some groups in China advocate for formal, as well as de facto, independence from China.

Ann Telnaes editiorial cartoon used with permission of Ann Telnaes and the Cartoonist Group. All rights reserved.

officials, Fukuoka officials, and representatives from Thailand and Mongolia. The setting: A banquet hosted by the Fukuoka government for international representatives at the Kyushu National Museum.

Sharing a table throughout the banquet, it was only after they exchanged business cards that Wu realized that Hsiao was a member of the pro-independence DPP. Initially taken aback, Wu then said that a recent visit to China by Kaohsiung Mayor Chen Chu—also a DPP member—was a first step in convincing the party to abandon Taiwanese sovereignty. Hsiao is then reported to have said that Chen's visit would not change the DPP's stance on independence, at least not until China had removed the 1,400 missiles or so it continues to aim at Taiwan (yes, despite all the cross-strait love we keep reading about in international media).

151

China Still Threatens

According to Hsiao's recollection, Wu then replied with the following: "What would retracting the missiles do? We can hit you even if we pull the missiles all the way back to Beijing. We not only have short-range missiles, we have plenty of mid-range ones, too."

And:

[The DPP] has done its thing for eight years, but didn't [former president] Chen Shui-bian end up in jail?[2] What international space? Ma Ying-jeou accepts the 'One China' principle, so we give him international space. The DPP wants independence for Taiwan and that is a dead-end road. You [Hsiao] are not even from the academic field, so what are you doing here? The DPP is a futureless party, unless it accepts One China.[3]

Hsiao then did what more Taiwanese should do under such circumstances: She put Wu on the spot, not by reciprocating hatred, not by screaming, but by translating, into English, Wu's comments for the benefit of the audience.

China Must Be Exposed

All is well in the Taiwan Strait? Think again. If the rest of the world won't believe Ma's detractors or refuse to at least listen to what the DPP and other pro-independence movements have to say, well, what else can be done but to allow Chinese officials to share their thoughts publicly? This was a brilliant coup, an extemporary one at that. More of the same is needed, which calls for a greater presence of DPP officials at public functions internationally, and highlights the dire need for English language abilities within the party so that such things can be communicated with the audience.

2. Chen Shui-bian was detained on corruption charges at the end of 2008.
3. One China is official Chinese policy toward Taiwan, which rejects formal Taiwanese independence.

This is what is needed, intelligent, rational exposure of the Chinese threat—not headline-grabbing, though ultimately pointless, antics such as the three DPP Taipei City Councilors who around the same time last month slapped white paint onto a KMT[4] symbol on the East Gate in Taipei.

Wu is no aberration; there are more where he came from. Despite what the rest of the world is being told, despite the so-called "peace" in the Taiwan Strait, China remains a bully and will not hesitate to threaten, even when things are going its way. The only reason we have been hearing about "peace" in the Taiwan Strait since Ma came into office a little more than a year ago is that unlike the DPP, his government has allowed itself to be intimidated by China's saber rattling.

---

4. The KMT is the party of Taiwanese president Ma Ying-jeou. It advocates for better relations with China.

> *"Fear of invasion by China in [Taiwan] is ebbing."*

China-Taiwan Relations Are Improving

Clifford Coonan

Clifford Coonan is a journalist based in Beijing. In the following viewpoint, he reports on the thaw in relations between China and the nearby island of Taiwan, which is self-governing but which has long been claimed by China. Coonan notes many signs of improved relations, from concrete trade agreements to symbolic gestures, such as the gift of two pandas from China to Taiwan. Coonan says that the improved relations are in large part the result of the election of President Ma Ying-jeou, who has backed away from demands for formal Taiwanese independence.

As you read, consider the following questions:

1. As cited by the author, during what period did China constantly bombard Taiwan?

2. When was martial law lifted in Taiwan, as described by Coonan?

3. As explained by the author, what do *Tuan Tuan* and *Yuan Yuan* said together mean in Chinese?

A shuddering explosion is an odd way of illustrating closer relations between self-ruled Taiwan and China, but clearing landmines from the beaches of Kinmen, a few hundred metres from the mainland, is a powerful symbol of how ties are getting ever closer.

Meanwhile, in Taipei zoo [in Taiwan], pandas Tuan Tuan and Yuan Yuan, probably the two most politicised animals in the world, happily munch on bamboo as Taiwanese flock to marvel at their antics. China gifted the two bears to Taiwan as a symbol of warmer relations.

Getting to Taiwan from Beijing used to involve a tedious stopover in Hong Kong, but now there are dozens of direct flights, and mainland tourists are much in evidence in the National Museum, home to most of the treasures of the Forbidden City[1], which Chiang Kai-shek's Kuomintang took with them when fleeing to the island in 1949 after they lost the civil war to Mao Zedong's Communists.

Fear Has Diminished

The demining process on Kinmen's beaches is a sign that fear of invasion by China in this island of 23 million is ebbing.

Kinmen has many tunnels, and in the central command area underground, a painting to commemorate the 60th anniversary of the Guningtou battle when the Chinese Communists invaded. This spot is just 8km from the mainland, and between 1954 and 1978 there was constant bombardment of the area by the mainlanders, who rained down two million shells on the island, 480,000 of them in the first two days of the bombing.

Some 30,000 artillery shells fell in 30 minutes. A local craftsman, Tseng-dong Wu, has developed a business making

---

1. The Forbidden City was the Chinese imperial palace located in Beijing.

Ma Ying-jeou Elected

Ma Ying-jeou, . . . who advocates better relations with China, was elected president of Taiwan by an overwhelming margin Saturday [March 22, 2008], opening the prospect of lowered tensions in the volatile Taiwan Strait. . . .

The results were likely to be greeted with a sigh of relief in Beijing, which claims this self-ruled island as a part of China but is eager to avoid a showdown that could lead to military conflict. They were also seen as welcome news in Washington, which has pledged to help Taiwan defend itself but would be reluctant to confront a crisis in Asia at a time when it is absorbed by conflicts in Iraq and Afghanistan.

Edward Cody, Washington Post, *March 22, 2008.*

high-precision cooking knives from the shell casings that litter the island. The scale of the assault makes it clear why the Taiwanese are so worried about the hundreds of missiles that remain pointed towards Taiwan.

Beijing has always threatened to use force to bring the self-governed island under mainland control if it declared formal independence. The US has promised to intervene if China attacks, and Washington is watching developments in the [Taiwan] Strait closely.

To prepare for what has looked like an inevitable follow-up invasion, the Taiwanese laid thousands of mines, mostly anti-personnel landmines, and installed networks of spikes on the beaches to stop landing craft. But the growing thaw across the Strait, efforts to boost the tourism potential of the island and pledges to meet international anti-landmine agreements mean the area is being demined.

"We won't be putting these mines back. Our concern now is demining and the area's development needs. All of the fields will be cleared 100 per cent by 2013 and we are planting trees, which act as a natural obstacle," said Lieutenant General Lu Xiao-rong.

Improved Ties with China

President Ma Ying-jeou, whose KMT party has been in office [since 2008], believes his efforts to improve ties with China have helped bring peace to the region.

Relations between China and Taiwan were strained under his predecessor Chen Shui-bian, who had a firmly pro-independence stance, much to the irritation of Beijing.

Mr Ma has made a top priority of improving ties with China. "In one year, we have transformed the Strait from a dangerous flashpoint to a conduit of peace and prosperity. We have a diplomatic truce with the mainland in the international arena and shelved 60 years of military conflict," he said at a briefing for foreign journalists in the presidential palace.

At the news conference, the Harvard-educated leader regularly came down from the podium to listen to journalists' questions close-up.

His open, engaging manner has done much to break down the lingering authoritarian image of the KMT party.

The KMT ran Taiwan effectively as a dictatorship until 1987 when martial law was lifted. Chen Shui-bian's Democratic Progressive Party (DPP) was elected in 2000, and the KMT found themselves out of power for the first time since 1949.

Under Mr Ma's stewardship, Beijing and Taipei have signed nine agreements on economic co-operation, including deals on direct flights and other trade deals. Taiwan has even been given tacit approval by Beijing to take part in international bodies such as the World Health Organisation.

There is also discussion again of the "One Country, Two Systems" model, which would allow Taiwan to remain democratic as part of the People's Republic, similar to the situation in Hong Kong.

However, the opposition believes Mr Ma's policies are endangering the island's sovereignty, and over half a million people demonstrated on Taipei's streets against the growing rapprochement across the Strait.

Pandas for Peace

In Taipei zoo, Tuan Tuan and Yuan Yuan, whose names said together mean "reunion" in Chinese and who have to count as the world's cuddliest-looking ambassadors, are blissfully unaware of their weighty diplomatic responsibilities.

So too are visitors to the zoo.

"They are very cute. We're very happy that they're here," said Wang Qian-yong, from Taipei.

"I don't really think about the political aspect."

Pandas are China's national symbol, and Tuan Tuan and Yuan Yuan have serious diplomatic muscle.

Beijing has a long history of using pandas in international relations, and for its part Taiwan has spared no expense in ensuring the comfort of the two four-year-olds, whose home was destroyed in the Sichuan earthquake in May [2008].

Up to 20,000 visitors a day come to see the pair at weekends. Their enclosure cost nearly €7 million [7 million euro], while a staff of 35 zookeepers plus a team of volunteers looks after them in their 765 sq m garden, complete with a playground, behind 4cm-thick soundproofed glass.

"The strengthened glass is for safety reasons," said Jason Ching, a research officer at the zoo. He is speaking beneath a portrait of Chiang Kai-shek, whose image has been restored to many public buildings since the KMT were returned to power. Under Chen Shui-bian's rule, Chiang Kai-shek was not a popular symbol.

"We had one demonstration outside the enclosure, with a person holding up a protest banner, but it was fine. Anyway, this is Taiwan, we're a democracy. You're allowed to say what you want," said Mr Ching.

Periodical Bibliography

The following articles have been selected to supplement the diverse views presented in this chapter.

Jayshree Bajoria	"The China–North Korea Relationship," Council on Foreign Relations, July 21, 2009. www.cfr.org.
BBC News	"China Fury at US Military Report," March 26, 2009. http://news.bbc.co.uk.
China Daily	"China Not a Threat: Australia," May 27, 2009. www2.chinadaily.com.cn.
Lisa Curtis	"China's Military and Security Relationship with Pakistan," Heritage Foundation, May 26, 2009. www.heritage.org.
Barbara Demick	"China Debates Its Bond with North Korea," *Los Angeles Times*, May 27, 2009. http://articles.latimes.com.
Cassie Fleming	"China's Military Buildup Worries Taiwan," *Washington Times*, July 16, 2009. www.washingtontimes.com.
Robert D. Kaplan	"When North Korea Falls," *Atlantic*, October 2006. www.theatlantic.com.
Thom Shanker	"U.S. Sees China Military Rise," *New York Times*, March 26, 2009. www.nytimes.com.
Stratfor	"China: The White Paper and Military Operations Abroad," January 23, 2009. www.stratfor.com.
John J. Tkacik	"America's Adversaries, China's Friends," *Washington Times*, July 16, 2009. www.washingtontimes.com.

OPPOSING
VIEWPOINTS®
SERIES

CHAPTER 4

Is China Protecting the Environment?

Chapter Preface

China's Communist government has a tradition of secrecy; the country's media is largely state run, and controversial information is released to the public slowly or not at all. The unwillingness to release information can be dangerous during a crisis involving the environment.

In 2003, a respiratory illness known as severe acute respiratory syndrome (SARS) developed in China. By the time the disease had run its course, more than five thousand people had been infected in China and more than three hundred had died. Worldwide there were nearly eight hundred deaths.

China's reaction to the SARS epidemic was initially to say as little as possible. According to Shanthi Kalathil writing in the *International Herald Tribune*, the Chinese government thought "that allowing information about the viral disease to circulate could contribute to social instability." This refusal to admit the problem had dire results, and was widely blamed for contributing to the severity of the spread both within China and worldwide. Hannah Beech, reporting in *Time*, noted that in Beijing "doctors had not been adequately schooled in infectious-disease protocol, since Beijing was still denying the capital had a SARS problem." The lack of preparation contributed to a failure of quarantine procedures and a spread of SARS among hospital workers. In addition, as the government was finally forced to admit the scope of the problem, panic spread through Beijing. Businesses closed, the economy ground to a halt, and people fled the city in droves. Beech noted that "the social stability that China's leaders were trying to maintain when they underplayed Beijing's SARS numbers has been shaken."

China's government did learn from the SARS debacle. In 2009, China reacted to the worldwide outbreak of a disease known as swine flu by initiating aggressive quarantine measures and reporting new cases swiftly. Hans Troedsson, head of the World Health Organization's Beijing Office, was quoted by the Associated Press as calling China's response to swine flu a "massive improvement" over its response to SARS.

China has clearly decided that, when dealing with infectious diseases, social stability is best served by transparency. But in other situations, officials still may respond by trying to shut down information or cover up problems. In 2009, for example, a scandal involving contaminated milk resulted in more than a thousand infant illnesses. China was slow to issue a recall of milk products, only taking action after being pressed by New Zealand, which had imported contaminated milk. New Zealand prime minister Helen Clark was quoted on the Javno Web site as noting that there had been an effort "for weeks" to initiate a recall, but that "the local authorities in China would not do it." She added, "I think the first inclination was to try and put a towel over it and deal with it without an official recall."

Similarly, in response to the massive earthquake in May 2008, which killed as many as eighty thousand, China's government was initially transparent, allowing national and international media coverage of damage and casualties. Soon, however, questions began to be raised about the shoddy construction possibly caused by construction; an unusual number of school buildings had collapsed in the quake, killing as many as ten thousand children. Instead of investigating these claims, the government refused to release information and began actively "intimidating parents and relatives of the child victims, who face harassment and arrest as they seek justice for the dead and injured," according to Clifford Coonan in an article in the *Independent*. Thus, in issues involving the health and safety of its people as well as of the environment, China continues to vacillate between greater transparency and its inclination toward secrecy.

> "*The global economic slowdown is help-ing to ... rein in the insatiable demand for coal-powered energy that ... has turned [China] into one of the world's most polluted nations.*"

China's Air Pollution Is Improving

Tini Tran

Tini Tran is a veteran foreign correspondent with the Associated Press. In the following viewpoint, she reports that pollution has fallen significantly in China. Partly this is due to controls put in place in the run-up to the 2008 Beijing Olympics, but mostly, Tran says, it is because of the economic slowdown. The fall in production, which has cleared the air in the short term, may also allow a move to cleaner technologies and the closing of old plants. This could result in long-term reductions in pollution, Tran notes.

As you read, consider the following questions:

1. The United Nations reported that carbon monoxide levels fell by how much during the two-week Olympics in Beijing, as cited by Tran?

Tini Tran, "Olympics, Economy Give China Cleanest Air In a Decade," Associated Press, April 4, 2009. Reprinted with permission of the Associated Press.

2. What air pollution index level is considered unhealthy for sensitive groups, as noted by the author?

3. As described by Tran, with production down 75 percent at Beijing Famed Machinery, what has owner Xu Demin decided to focus his energy on?

Last summer [2008], Xu Demin struggled to cut emissions from his coal-fired factories as part of China's all-out effort to clean the air for the Beijing Olympics.

He could have simply waited six months. This spring, overseas demand for his farming and construction machinery plummeted, forcing him to close two plants and lay off 300 workers.

The global economic slowdown is helping to accomplish what some in China's leadership have striven to do for years: rein in the insatiable demand for coal-powered energy that has fed the country's breakneck growth but turned it into one of the world's most polluted nations.

Bad Economy, Better Pollution

Beijing, China's normally smog-choked capital, is breathing some of its cleanest air in nearly a decade, as pollution-control efforts get a sizable boost from a slowing economy.

"It's like the sky I saw overseas. I can see clouds. I've seen days here like I've seen in Europe or the U.S.," Xu says, his voice echoing in the cavernous space of his idle factory outside Beijing.

An Associated Press analysis of government figures backs up his observations: In the second half of last year, a period that included the Olympics in August, Beijing recorded its lowest air pollution readings since 2000, according to data from the Ministry of Environmental Protection.

The average monthly air pollution index was 74, about 25 percent lower than the previous seven years. Earlier data were not available.

Experts see several reasons for the improvement, including the relocation of some of Beijing's dirtiest factories outside the city and the partial continuation of traffic limits imposed for the Olympics.

Perhaps most significant has been the economic downturn. Even elsewhere in China, where no Olympic pollution measures were imposed, the level of dirty air is down.

Chak Chan, who has published studies on China's air quality, warns the relief offered by the slump is temporary. "But if taken as an opportunity to do more in terms of energy efficiency and clean technology, then it can have a long-term effect in improving air quality," said Chan, a professor at Hong Kong University of Science and Technology.

For now, the cleaner air is a vindication of sorts for Beijing. China won its bid to host the Olympics partly on the promise that it would lead to a cleaner capital.

Olympics Spurred Reform

The government spent billions of dollars to clean up the air. It followed that spending with two months of drastic measures, temporarily shutting factories across five provinces, suspending construction in the capital, and ordering drivers to idle their cars every other day from July to September.

The results were dramatic, with air pollution index hitting record lows in August and September. Viewers around the world watched some sporting events take place under crystal blue skies.

In an assessment released in February [2009], the U.N. Environmental Program said carbon monoxide levels fell 47 percent and sulfur dioxide 38 percent during the two-week Olympics. Even Beijing's worst pollutant—tiny particles of dust, soot and aerosol known as particulate matter 10—was reduced by 20 percent. The U.N. report praised China for investing in long-term solutions such as public transport, urban parks and renewable-energy vehicles.

City officials also kept some traffic limits in place after the Olympics. Car owners are banned from driving one day a week, depending on their license plate numbers.

Air pollution, while not as low as in August and September when the harshest restrictions were in place, has remained far below recent years. From October through February, the average monthly pollution index was 82.

On a recent sunny morning, Li Heng, 66, joined dozens of seniors in Beijing's Ritan Park for a daily round of tai chi, the slow breathing exercises.

"I think the air is much better recently. We can take very deep breaths and the air feels fresh," he said, inhaling and exhaling loudly before thumping his chest.

It's not just Beijing. Southern China, home to many of the country's export-producing factories, has seen clear improvement.

Many cities in Guangdong province, where 62,400 businesses closed [in 2007], have seen a drop in the number of badly polluted days, according to data on the Guangdong Provincial Environmental Protection Bureau Web site.

For example, the factory city of Dongguan reported more than a dozen days in the first half of 2008 when the air pollution index topped 100, a level considered unhealthy for sensitive groups including infants and the elderly. But in the second half of the year, there were only two such days.

Not all cities saw improvements. But across a sampling of seven key cities, the average number of badly polluted days halved between the first and second half of 2008.

A similar phenomenon was seen when the Soviet Union collapsed, causing the industrial haze over the Arctic to drop by nearly 50 percent, said Kenneth Rahn, an atmospheric chemist from the University of Rhode Island who has studied air quality in China.

China Targets Cars

Beijing is so desperate to get high-polluting cars off the roads, the city has devised a scheme that will pay citizens as much as $3600 to give up heavily polluting vehicles— and even give drivers more money to purchase cleaner cars.

The [2009] initiative would take about 10 percent of the city's 3.5-million registered cars off the roads—an amount that is estimated to account for 50 percent of the city's notorious vehicle pollution.

Alex Pasternack. www.causecast.org.

"In principle, a reduction in economic activity can and will reduce air pollution," he wrote in an e-mail response. "I would expect something similar for China but of lesser magnitude."

Long-Term Improvement

During boom times, demand for electricity was so high in Guangdong's Pearl River Delta that companies often endured rotating blackouts. Some installed their own generators, which burned low-grade, dirty fuel.

But since last fall [2008], blackouts have been few, and generators are seldom used.

Environmental advocates say the downturn presents an opportunity for the government to move more aggressively to shut the dirtiest plants and enact stricter emissions regulations.

"The fact that the economy has slowed down has made it easier to stick to their plans to consolidate and close plants," said Deborah Seligsohn, director of the China climate program for the U.S-based World Resources Institute.

Seligsohn said she is encouraged by the fact that China's $586 billion economic stimulus plan includes funding for better technology and infrastructure that could benefit the environment.

In Guangdong, the slowdown could spur long-held plans to transform the region from dirty, labor-intensive manufacturing to cleaner high-tech industries.

Wang Xiaoming, director of communication for the Beijing Environmental Protection Bureau, said he hopes companies will take advantage of the slowdown to install more energy-efficient and cleaner technology.

"This period is an opportunity for each factory to adjust their production methods. If they were operating at full capacity, they would never have the time for this," he said.

It's advice that Xu, 59, has taken to heart as he seeks to reinvent Beijing Famed Machinery, his two-decade-old company.

With production down 75 percent this year, he has now decided to focus his energy on what had largely been a side project: making and selling machines that turn agricultural waste into what he calls "green coal"—fuel pellets that burn more cleanly than coal.

"It's up to us whether we can turn crisis into opportunity," he said. "This is a good time for our biomass product."

The longtime business owner even draws inspiration from the late founding father of communist China: "As Chairman Mao said, under certain circumstances, the bad thing can lead to a good result."

| "New data on the ... implications of China's pollution ... call for more serious efforts by global stakeholders to engage China on these issues."

China Must Do More to Address Air Pollution

Juli S. Kim

Juli S. Kim is the China Program coordinator at Conservation International. In the following viewpoint, she argues that China's air pollution is a serious and growing problem for China itself, for its neighbors, and even for distant nations such as the United States. Kim contends that Chinese air pollution causes serious health problems and economic losses both within and outside China. Kim suggests that the United States and other nations need to do more to encourage China to confront air pollution, and that China needs to do more to address the problem.

As you read, consider the following questions:

1. According to Kim, the majority of China's air pollution originates from the country's heavy dependence on what?

Juli S. Kim, "A China Environmental Health Project Research Brief: Transboundary Air Pollution—Will China Choke on Its Own Success," Woodrow Wilson Center, February 2, 2007. Reproduced by permission.

2. According to the World Bank, as cited by the author, how many people in China die every year due to respiratory illness triggered by pollution?

3. How much of the world's mercury emissions come from Asia, according to Kim?

It is difficult to understate the influence of China's atmospheric pollution on the Asia Pacific region and beyond. Prevailing winds carry pollutants such as ozone, fine particulate matter, and mercury from continent to continent, and in this case, from Asia to North America. Although statistics on China's dismal air quality are dated, anecdotal, or limited in scope (e.g., China has not publicly disclosed CO_2 or mercury emissions data since 2001), when examined as a whole, overall air pollution trends indicate a growing economic and health threat both within and outside China. Although the regional impact of China's air pollution has encouraged some cooperation, new data on the economic, environmental, and human health implications of China's pollution on Northeast Asia and the western seaboard of the United States and Canada call for more serious efforts by global stakeholders to engage China on these issues.

Coal, Cars, and Desertification

The majority of China's domestic and transboundary air pollution originates from the country's heavy dependence on coal, which makes up about 70 percent of its energy mix. Despite efforts to diversify energy sources, China will remain dependent upon coal for the foreseeable future. This dependence—along with the low quality of the coal, the lack of widespread coal washing infrastructure and scrubbers at industrial facilities and power plants, and plans for building nearly 100 new coal-fired power stations each year until 2012—translate into increasing health and environmental problems for the East Asia/Pacific region and beyond. China is second only to the United States in energy consumption and greenhouse gas (GHG) emissions, and is expected to surpass the United States in GHG emissions by 2009. The expansion of China's power plants alone could nullify the cuts required under the Kyoto Protocol[1] from industrialized countries.

Beyond coal, in urban centers where the majority of the wealth and record breaking GDP[2] rates are generated, car emissions have replaced coal as the major source of air pollution. Currently, sixteen of the world's twenty most polluted cities are in China and auto emissions will worsen urban air quality in China. Although current data show that China only has 22 cars per 1,000 people as opposed to 764 per 1,000 in the United States—China is well on its way to becoming the dominant market for automobiles. As vehicles become more affordable, due especially to WTO [World Trade Organization] tariff reductions, the number of automobiles in China is expected to rise from the current 24 million to 100 million by 2020. There is already a car culture developing, similar to that witnessed in the United States during the 1940s, with car driving clubs as a prime example. Policies for cleaner cars have been made, but face many obstacles. [Below are] more examples of the economic and health costs of China's growing air pollution.

- The average decrease in China's crop yield attributable to the combined effects of acid rain from SO_2 [sulfur dioxide] emissions and black carbon soot was 4.3 percent in the mid-1990s.

- Climate experts link greenhouse gas emissions and deforestation to the rising incidences of natural disasters witnessed between January and September of 2006, which forced the evacuation and relocation of 13.2 mil-

1. The Kyoto Protocol is a United Nations agreement on greenhouse gas reduction.
2. GDP, or gross domestic product, is a measure of all goods and services produced in a country.

lion people and killed more than 2,300, causing direct economic losses of $24 billion.

- According to recent estimates by Qin Dahe, director of the China Meteorological Administration, air pollution is driving some extreme weather events, which hamper China's economic growth by between 3 to 6 percent of GDP, or $70–130 billion, annually.

- Coal burning in China emits 25 percent of global mercury and 12 percent of global CO_2.

- A 2006 SEPA [Solar Electric Power Association] survey found that 41 percent of fish species in water bodies in eastern Jiangsu Province, where there is a high concentration of manufacturers, contained various heavy metals transmitted through polluted air fall-out.

- SEPA estimates that nearly 200 cities in China fall short of the WHO standards for airborne particulates.

Exacerbating the coal and car emission pollutants are large plumes of dust the size of small countries blowing eastward from the encroaching deserts of Mongolia and Western China. Desertification in China is advancing at an annual rate of 1,300 square miles, destroying farmlands and driving more rural migrants into cities. The expanding deserts are increasing the severity of the spring sandstorms—100 are expected between 2000 and 2009, a significant increase over the 23 in the previous decade. Regionally, sulfur dioxide (SO_2) and mercury emissions from coal burning are some of the main pollutants spreading from China. Acid rain resulting from coal and fossil fuel combustion has been damaging nearly one-third of China's limited cropland. The Korean Peninsula and Japan have felt the brunt of China's "export" through acid rain, mercury, and other airborne contaminants as Siberian winds and dust storms flush out China's pollution every spring, severely damaging forests and watersheds.

More recently, studies have examined the problems associated with black carbon (BC) soot in China. BC—the active ingredient in haze produced by burning crop residues, household coal stoves, and vehicles—is potentially the second most potent global warming gas after CO_2. China is the largest BC emitting country in the world, responsible for 17 percent of these emissions. The BC particles are less than one micron in diameter and cause hundreds of thousands of premature deaths from respiratory illnesses each year in China. Moreover, BC blocks sunlight and may be lowering crop yields for both wheat and rice in China by 30 percent. Regionally, scientists consider China's BC emissions as responsible for some of the warming and destabilizing weather throughout the Pacific Rim.

The Health Effect

According to a recent World Bank report, some 300,000 to 400,000 people die in China every year due to respiratory illnesses triggered by air pollution. Globally, scientific research is illuminating the clear linkages between not only air pollution and respiratory complications, but also to heart disease. For example, a study in *Heart*, the journal of the British Cardiac Society, found a corollary relationship between increases in particulate air pollution and deaths from heart diseases. A study funded in part by the U.S. Environmental Protection Agency in *The New England Journal of Medicine* features one of the largest studies ever conducted on the linkages between heart diseases, stroke, and air pollution. This particular study, which focused on women, found air quality to be a strong predictor of heart and stroke risks. However, experts claim that although it is indisputable that fine particle air pollutants pose a risk to health, the reasons are not quite as clear. Researchers state they are still investigating whether it is the chemical composition, size, or ability to transport other pollutants deep into the lungs that is responsible for the effect.

These particles often measure less than one-tenth of a micron, in essence being small enough to pass through the walls of a human lung, into the body's red blood cells. In one study in the *Journal of Toxicology and Environmental Health*, researchers found that in the developing nations of Asia two-thirds of their health problems are due to urban air pollution. The growing level of mercury in the air and water in China also raises major health concerns. Mercury accumulates in living tissue, such as fish grown in China's numerous aquaculture pools. When this fish is eaten it can cause birth defects, child development problems, and potentially cancer.

Disappearing GDP Effect

In 2006, China's environmental watchdog echoed the 1997 World Bank's *Clear Air Blue Water* report that domestic health problems and economic losses stemming from pollution cost China nearly 8 percent of the GDP—statistically eating up almost all of the country's economic growth. The Chinese government's *Green National Accounting Study Report* claims that pollution in general is cutting into 3.1 percent of GDP—although other economists place the number as high as 10 percent.

In China an estimated 19 percent of the agricultural land in seven southern provinces (Jiangsu, Zhejiang, Anhui, Fujian, Hunan, Hubei, and Jiangxi) has been damaged by SO_2 and acid rain. Additionally, China's dirty production is also very detrimental to Hong Kong's economy. A group of nine public health researchers, economists, and environmental scientists released a report in June 2006 estimating that air pollution—much of it blowing from the north—could cost Hong Kong as much as HK$21 billion a year.

Investors also are coming to view this pollution [as] a concern. Independently, both the chairman of the Hong Kong Stock Exchange and Merrill Lynch issued media-grabbing statements that the worsening air quality in southern China is a threat to Hong Kong's economic competitiveness. The problems lie directly upwind in the Pearl River Delta, where one-third of China's exports are produced, as well as 80 percent of Hong Kong's air pollution. As the number of days with reduced visibility has tripled in the past three years, a recent survey discovered that 40 percent of businesses were finding it harder to recruit overseas nationals to Hong Kong and southern China due to this factor. In response, Merrill Lynch's Asia Pacific division recently suggested that investors should sell properties in Hong Kong and invest in Singapore instead. Additionally, Merrill Lynch criticized the Hong Kong government's lack of willpower to deal with the pollution problems, especially as most feel that waiting for Beijing to enact tougher laws and enforcement will be a long wait indeed.

China's Invisible Export

The byproducts of China's development are now being felt as far as the east coast of the United States. Besides the aforementioned statistics on China's contribution to global warming and regional mercury fallout—research by the UN now indicates that some 53 percent of the world's natural and human caused mercury emissions come from Asia, while Africa is a distant second with only 18 percent. The most commonly cited numbers attribute between 25 and 40 percent of global mercury emissions (from coal burning) to China. Within China's borders, air pollution from coal, cars, and dust storms is responsible for between 300,000 and 400,000 premature deaths and 75 million asthma attacks annually. Additionally, China's cement kilns, which account for around 40 percent of global cement production, are a major source of dioxin and furan—pollutants that can be transported airborne across long distances.

High levels of mercury deposition in the United States from China and India had been detected on both coasts of the

Air Pollution in 2008

Particulate air pollution during the 2008 Olympic Games in Beijing constantly exceeded levels considered excessive by the World Health Organization, was far worse than other recent Olympic Games, and was about 30 percent higher than has been reported by Chinese environmental experts—even though some favorable weather conditions helped reduce the problem. . . .

The levels were about two to four times higher than that of Los Angeles on an average day.

Red Orbit, June 19, 2009. www.redorbit.com.

United States. Research conducted in Oregon has shown that one-fifth of the mercury entering the Williamette River in Oregon comes from abroad, mostly from China. Mercury is especially suited for long distance travel because at the smoke-stack in China it is in elemental form and insoluble. However, by the time it reaches the U.S. west coast, it has transformed into a reactive gaseous material that dissolves in Oregon's wet climate—falling onto the Williamette River's watershed and slowly building up toxic levels of mercury in the local wildlife.

Mercury is just one transboundary pollutant that U.S. scientists are tracking. Bruce Hope, a senior environmental toxicologist at the Oregon Department of Environmental Quality, estimates that global sources contribute 18 percent—more than four times the local share—to Oregon's air pollution. Increasingly, the ozone on the west coast will be determined by China. In California, for example, some researchers believe at least one-third of California's fine particulate pollution—known as aerosol—originates from Asia. These pollutants could potentially nullify California's progress on meeting stricter Clean Air Act requirements. In May 2006, University of California-Davis researchers claimed that almost all the particulate matter over Lake Tahoe was from China. The great irony is that these pollutants are mainly due to the burgeoning demand of U.S. and EU [European Union] consumers for cheap Chinese goods—which is driving the Chinese economic development. Some estimates cite that 7 percent of China's CO_2 emissions are due to production of U.S. imports.

Cooperative Collaboration

The Chinese government has welcomed considerable international assistance to help the country address its severe air pollution problems that are tied to coal mining, cars, and desertification. The international community—in the form of multilateral organizations, bilateral aid, and nongovernmental organizations [NGOs]—has been very active in addressing a broad range of air pollution issues through energy efficiency, demand-side management, clean coal, and renewable energy projects. Many of these projects have been driven by international concern regarding China's growing GHG emissions, but nearly all of them focus on local benefits of controlling such emissions.

While U.S. NGOs are particularly active in energy and air pollution collaboration in China, the U.S. government could have more sustained projects in these areas. The growing . . . regional impacts of China's air pollution and related energy hunger should be viewed as incentives for the [George W.] Bush administration and Congress to pursue active environmental collaboration with China—before China's energy hunger and pollution—which is in large part due to U.S. and EU consumerism—are used as political tools to vilify China. There is a definite need to develop a coherent approach to energy and environmental relations with China. As the April 2000 spy-plane incident and recent [January 2007] satellite shootdown illustrated, there remains considerable mistrust between the United States and China—cooperation on energy and environmental issues could help build up needed trust between the two countries.

The Chinese government has shown initiative through recent enactments of stricter air pollution control laws and major new incentives and investments into renewable energy, however, the need for the conveyance of a clear and cohesive strategy, along with coordination and organization throughout all the ministries and environmental protection bureaus is necessary for China to begin to balance the benefits of economic growth against the negative costs of air pollution to public health.

| "China has. . . [begun] to make environmental improvements."

China Is Addressing Climate Change

Steven Hayward

Steven Hayward is senior fellow at the Pacific Research Institute and a resident scholar at the American Enterprise Institute. In the following viewpoint, Steven Hayward asserts that China is working at "breakneck speed" to address its environmental problems. Although there is a lot of pessimism surrounding China's relationship to the environment, Hayward argues that China is beginning to address climate change by taking steps to implement better technology to reduce pollution, as well as enacting many environmental laws. While China is roughly where the United States was in 1950 in terms of environmental performance, Hayward is optimistic that China's environmental news is going to start improving a lot sooner and faster than people expect.

As you read, consider the following questions:

1. How many of China's major cities fail to meet the nation's air quality standards, according to the viewpoint?

Steven Hayward, "China Comes Clean," *National Review*, April 21, 2006. Reproduced by permission.

2. What are some of the ways in which China is addressing climate change, as listed in the viewpoint?

3. According to the viewpoint, how is China doing in environmental performance as compared to the United States?

It is the fashion these days to apply the overused phrase the "tipping point" to just about everything, especially when it comes to bad news for the environment. And nowhere is the pessimism greater than when it comes to China, whose spectacular economic growth and voracious appetite for natural resources is said to be leading the region and perhaps the world toward irreversible ecological catastrophe.

This story line, played out in countless media headlines over the past few years, has it backwards. China has indeed reached a tipping point on the environment—the point at which it begins to make environmental improvements.

China's Environmental Problems

It's about time. China has some of the worst pollution problems in the world. Nearly two-thirds of China's 343 major cities currently fail to meet the nation's air quality standards. The World Health Organization reckons that seven of the ten most polluted cities in the world are in China. Pollution levels in China's major cities are 10 to 50 times higher than the worst smoggy day in Los Angeles.

The story is much the same with water pollution. China is desperately short of potable water. Groundwater has been badly depleted, and surface water sources are equally overused. The Yellow River, for example, has run dry every year since 1985 because of diversions; in 1997, it failed to reach the ocean for 226 days. Severe water pollution has led to shutdowns of major urban water systems, such as occurred last year in the city of Harbin following a chemical spill in the

Songhua River. The city of 3.8 million people was without running water for nearly a week.

These and other environmental trends are supposedly going to get worse as China continues its headlong drive to become a modern industrial nation. "China's Next Big Boom Could Be the Foul Air," the *New York Times* reported last October [2005]. Yet these predictions are already out of date. A look at the data shows that China is on the curve that other modern industrialized nations followed in the mid-20th century, whereby pollution starts to fall even as the economy continues to grow. Sulfur dioxide and particulate levels have actually fallen in Beijing and other major cities over the last decade, at the same time as the number of motor vehicles China nearly quadrupled and total energy consumption increased by one-third.

China Is Addressing Its Environmental Problems

China is slowly turning the corner on the environment for the same reason the U.S. and other advanced economies reversed course a generation ago—economic growth provides the means to implement better technology to reduce pollution. China has been enacting environmental laws that resemble the landmark legislation the U.S. and Europe enacted in the 1970s, and China's State Environmental Protection Administration (SEPA) reports that spending for environmental projects is increasing about 15 percent a year. China has adopted the European Union's automobile tailpipe standards, for example, and has even begun to emulate our Environmental Impact Review process for major construction projects.

China is working at breakneck speed to reverse its water pollution and supply problems as well. Industrial discharge of petroleum-related pollutants and heavy metals into rivers and oceans has been cut in half over the last decade. Wastewater treatment facilities are quickly being built; between 2000 and

Statistics Relevant to Climate Change for China and the U.S.	China	United States
Population (millions)	1,305	297
Population growth (annual %)	0.6	1.0
Gross domestic product (billions US$)	2,244	12,398
GDP growth (%)	10.4	3.2
Energy consumption per capita (kg oil equivalent per capita)	1,316	7,893
Electricity consumption per capita (kWh per capita)	1,718	13,698
Greenhouse gas emissions (metric tons CO_2e)	7,527	7,282
Greenhouse gas emissions per capita (metric tons per capita)	6	25
Greenhouse gas emissions per GNI (tons per 1,000 US$ GNI, using purchasing power parities)	1.4	0.6

TAKEN FROM: Jane A. Leggett, Jeffrey Logan, and Anna Mackey, "CRS Report for Congress: China's Greenhouse Gas Emissions and Mitigation Policies," *Federation of American Scientists Web site*, September 10, 2008.

2005, total wastewater capacity doubled. China's reforestation program appears to be taking flight; SEPA reports that 4.8 million hectares of forestland were planted in 2004, and that forestland has been growing at slightly more than 1 percent a year over the last decade.

China Today

China today is roughly where the United States was in 1950 terms of environmental performance. In those days the U.S. still poured raw sewage and chemicals directly into rivers and lakes and the ocean, and had little along the lines of air pollution controls. Like the U.S. 50 years ago, China has a long way to go. Some of the environmental news out of China is going to get worse before it gets better. The central point remains, however, that China's environmental news is going to start improving a lot sooner and a lot faster than people expect.

The most intriguing possibility from this story is how environmental reform might contribute to political reform and liberalization. Many of the changes in China's environmental performance are coming in response to large public protests—and frequent riots—over pollution. The environment, often an anti-democratic force in American governance, might prove to be a tipping point toward democracy in China.

> *"If climate scientists are right about the narrow window of opportunity available to avoid catastrophic global warming, the world needs more from China."*

China Must Do More on Climate Change

Bruce Stokes

Bruce Stokes is the international economics columnist for the National Journal, *a Washington-based public policy magazine. In the following viewpoint, Stokes argues that China has not made as much progress in addressing climate change as its government claims. Stokes points out that, while China had taken some steps, it remains the largest source of greenhouse gas emissions in the world. Stokes contends that China must invest in cleaner technology and move toward a more service-oriented economy if there is to be any hope of addressing worldwide climate change.*

As you read, consider the following questions:

1. Between 2002 and 2005, according to Stokes, which grew faster in China, economic growth or energy demand?

2. How much of China's energy is derived from coal-fired generating plants, according to the author?

3. What does Stokes say may happen to green technology sold to China if intellectual property rights are not protected?

The first thing that strikes a visitor to the Taiyanggong natural-gas-fired, electrical co-generating plant is the low hum. The facility's two giant General Electric turbines produce only 55 decibels of sound, the noise level of a room air conditioner.

But it was clean, not quiet, power China sought when it built this plant in 2007 in northeast Beijing. Each year, Taiyanggong produces as much electricity as 78 low-efficiency, coal-fired boilers, and thereby cuts CO_2 [carbon dioxide, the major greenhouse gas] emissions by 60 percent. In addition, the project co-generates steam for heating a large portion of China's capital.

Little wonder that Taiyanggong is China's showcase generating plant. Secretary of State Hillary Rodham Clinton visited in February [2009]. But such Chinese endeavors, impressive as they may be, are deceptive.

With natural gas costing at least four times more than coal in China, plants such as Taiyanggong are a prohibitively expensive means of producing electricity. Even though Taiyanggong is 13 percent more efficient than the best-operating coal-powered generating facility, its high cost dictates that, nationwide, China continues to build dirtier coal plants at a pace of nearly two per week.

With the governments of the world meeting in Bonn [Germany] on June 1, [2009,] to begin the stretch run toward forging a new global climate pact by the end of the year, China is trying to convince outside observers that it is making great strides toward curbing global warming.

The reality, however, is that China still adds more CO_2 to the atmosphere each year than any other nation in the world. Moreover, Beijing rejects any binding international cap on such emissions and claims the right to continue to increase its release of greenhouse gases, albeit more slowly than before.

Operating on the assumption that more flies are caught with honey than vinegar, the [Barack] Obama administration has chosen to laud China's efforts rather than criticize its lack of ambition. Such a strategy makes for good diplomacy but bad environmental science. Unless China can be persuaded to begin reducing its CO_2 emissions soon, there is little prospect of halting global warming.

Chinese officials like to change the subject when they're confronted with complaints about the country's greenhouse-gas emissions. They point out that on a cumulative basis since 1800, China's emissions amount to a third of what the U.S. has produced. They note that the average Chinese still generates less than a quarter of the annual CO_2 emissions that an average American produces.

Such arguments are disingenuous. To the rapidly warming Earth's atmosphere, it matters little whether a greenhouse gas was released in 1909 or 2009, or whether it was generated by one American or four Chinese. Without a reduction in China's emissions, the world is going to become an uncomfortably warm place.

This forecast is not meant to slight Beijing's recent efforts to curb its carbon emissions. In many ways, it has done more than Washington has. China has fuel-economy standards that are more stringent than those in the U.S.: It required new vehicles to average 36.7 miles per gallon in 2008; new U.S. standards will require only 35.5 miles per gallon by 2016.

China has also embraced renewable energy. It gets about 17 percent of its electricity from renewable sources, such as wind and solar; the United States derives only 9 percent of its power from clean sources. China is already the world's leading

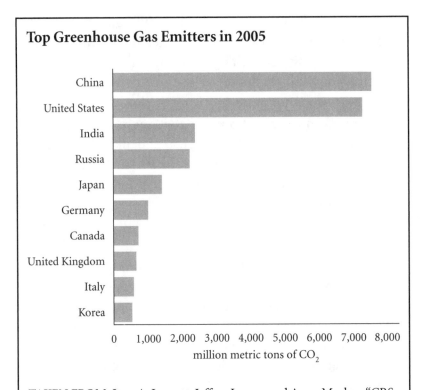

Top Greenhouse Gas Emitters in 2005

million metric tons of CO_2

TAKEN FROM: Jane A. Leggett, Jeffrey Logan, and Anna Mackey, "CRS Report for Congress: China's Greenhouse Gas Emissions and Mitigation Policies," *Federation of American Scientists Web site*, September 10, 2008.

producer of solar panels and solar water heaters. In 2008, Beijing doubled its installed wind capacity for the fourth straight year and is now the fourth-largest producer of wind power after the United States, Germany, and Spain. And China leads the world in dam-generated power.

Recognizing that conservation is the cleanest source of new energy, China is devoting a significant portion of its current economic stimulus spending to improving energy efficiency, especially in buildings.

Yet this impressive effort masks broader, more-troubling developments. China is still a woefully inefficient user of power. It requires four times as much energy as the U.S. needs to generate the same amount of economic growth, and nine times as much as Japan does. The energy intensity of the Chinese economy—the amount of power needed to add a dollar to economic growth—recently reversed itself after improving for decades. Between 2002 and 2005, energy demand here grew faster than economic growth, as investment in heavy manufacturing soared.

In the run-up to the international climate-change summit in Copenhagen in December [2009], China's efforts and its shortcomings deserve special scrutiny.

In climate negotiations to date, Beijing has proposed a business-as-usual approach, offering only to reduce the energy intensity of its economy, which would effectively return the country to the energy-efficiency path it was on before 2002. If climate scientists are right about the narrow window of opportunity available to avoid catastrophic global warming, the world needs more from China.

The place to start is power generation. China still derives about 70 percent of its electricity from coal-fired generating plants. Although the country is the world's leading builder of more-efficient, less-polluting coal facilities, only about three in five of those plants use clean technologies.

Furthermore, wrote Kenneth Lieberthal, a professor at the University of Michigan, and David Sandalow, a senior fellow at the Brookings Institution in Washington, in a paper earlier this year [2009], "specific problems often result in emissions far above the level that would be anticipated from plant technology alone. . . . Many operators purchase and burn low-quality coal that undermines the efficiency capabilities of the advanced technologies in their plants."

To improve its operations, China needs clean technology and better management of that capability once it is in place. The low-carbon energy lab at Tsinghua University here recently formed an alliance with Cambridge University in the United Kingdom and the Massachusetts Institute of Technology in the United States to begin developing such equipment.

More collaboration is needed, and scientists must work more closely with utilities, steelmakers, and others to ensure that design meshes with function.

But such efforts take time, and China needs clean technology now. To obtain that equipment from the West, Beijing would have to find the money to pay for it. Furthermore, the intellectual-property rights of the companies that own the technology must be protected so that it will not be copied and in turn sold to third countries.

This will not be easy. A business coalition led by the U.S. Chamber of Commerce and some major U.S. multinational companies has warned the Obama administration about giving away proprietary green technologies. And with China running a $266 billion trade surplus with the United States last year [2008], Congress is in no mood to pay for climate-friendly equipment for the Chinese.

Beijing must recognize that as long as it is sitting on $1.9 trillion in foreign reserves, the world will expect it to buy its own clean technology. Similarly, given China's abysmal record in protecting intellectual property, some sort of international arbitration or insurance scheme must be set up to guarantee technology holders their rights.

More broadly, China needs to accelerate its transition from an export-driven and manufacturing-dependent economy to a more domestically oriented, service-based model. Because Beijing seems reluctant to make this shift, it may need the encouragement of Western trade and exchange-rate policies that will make producing steel and dirty exports less attractive. But such leverage will have limited value as long as the Chinese do not commit themselves to a cleaner model of economic development.

The Taiyanggong plant and similar projects demonstrate that Beijing can curb its emissions. But much more is needed from China. And time is short.

Periodical Bibliography

The following articles have been selected to supplement the diverse views presented in this chapter.

David Biello	"Can Coal and Clean Air Coexist in China?" *Scientific American*, August 4, 2008. www.scientificamerican.com.
China Daily	"Water, Air Pollution in China Still Serious," February 24, 2009. www.chinadaily.net.
Eileen Claussen	"Roadmap for a U.S.-China Partnership on Climate Change," Pew Center on Global Climate Change, March 6, 2009. www.pewclimate.org.
Dan Fagin	"Is China's Pollution Poisoning Its Children?" *Scientific American*, August 2008. www.scientificamerican.com.
Holly Hart and John Frisbie	"Product Safety Is China's Achilles' Heel," *BusinessWeek*, October 29,2008. www.businessweek.com.
Mark Landler	"Clinton Paints China Policy with a Green Hue," *New York Times*, February 21, 2009. www.nytimes.com.
Brook Larmer	"Bitter Rivers," *National Geographic*, August 2009. http://ngm.nationalgeographic.com.
Don Lee	"China's Product Safety Agency Under Fire from Within," *Los Angeles Times*, August 30, 2008. http://articles.latimes.com.
Jonathan Watts	"China Dust Storm: Global Dimming Starts Here," *Guardian* (Manchester, U.K.), March 19, 2009. www.guardian.co.uk.
Lin Yang	"China's Three Gorges Dam Under Fire," *Time*, October 12, 2007. www.time.com.

For Further Discussion

Chapter 1

1. Imagine that China experienced a massive economic contraction. Would this make a change toward a freer government more or less likely, according to Henry S. Rowen? According to Arthur Kroeber? Explain the reasoning behind your answers, citing from those viewpoints.

2. Based on Amnesty International's report on China, do "normal religious activities" include all religious activities? What activities do not seem to be protected? Cite examples from the viewpoints in this chapter.

Chapter 2

1. Jeff Nielson accuses the U.S. financial press of deliberately trying to undermine faith in China's economy in order to make the U.S. economy look better. In his piece for the U.S. financial publication *Forbes*, does Nouriel Roubini argue that China's economy is weaker than that of the United States? Explain your answer.

2. James A. Dorn says "consumers gain regardless of why imports are cheap." According to Peter Navarro, why are imports cheap? Do you think it hurts Dorn's argument to discuss the specific reasons that imports are cheap? Explain.

3. Henry Blodget says, "The reason pirated products are so wildly popular is that customers *love* their value proposition." According to David Wolf, do customers love the value of all pirated products? Explain your answer.

Chapter 3

1. John J. Tkacik Jr. argues that the Chinese military buildup is meant to challenge China's neighbors and the United States. Would Doug Bandow consider this a legitimate Chinese goal? Explain your answers.

2. Does Anne Applebaum offer any direct evidence (such as quotes or statements from Chinese sources) that the Chinese are encouraging North Korean nuclear missile tests? If so, what evidence does she provide? Why might she argue that such evidence is not available?

Chapter 4

1. Bruce Stokes notes that between 2002 and 2005, energy demand in China grew faster than economic growth. Based on Tini Tran's viewpoint, is energy demand likely to continue to outpace growth in 2008–2009? Explain your answer.

Organizations to Contact

American Enterprise Institute (AEI)
1150 Seventeenth St. NW, Washington, DC   20036
(202) 862-5800
e-mail: vrodman@aei.org
Web site: www.aei.org

The institute is a conservative public policy research organization dedicated to preserving and strengthening government, private enterprise, foreign policy, and national defense. Its Asian Studies Program focuses on the growing offensive capabilities of China's army, relations between Taiwan and mainland China, and economic and political reform in China. AEI's magazine, *American Enterprise*, often deals with developments in Asia, and the institute also publishes several books on China.

Amnesty International (AI)
5 Penn Plaza, New York, NY   10001
(212) 807-8400 • fax: (212) 627-1451
e-mail: admin-us@aiusa.org
Web site: www.amnesty.org

This international organization works to promote human rights around the world. It posts updates on human rights issues and flashpoints on its Web site. It also publishes an annual report detailing human rights violations in many countries, including China.

The Asia Society
725 Park Ave., New York, NY   10021
(212) 288-6400 • fax: (212) 517-8315
e-mail: info@asiasociety.org
Web site: www.asiasociety.org

The Asia Society is an educational organization dedicated to fostering understanding of Asia and communication between Americans and the peoples of Asia and the Pacific. Reports and articles about China are available on its Web site.

Brookings Institution

1775 Massachusetts Ave. NW, Washington, DC   20036

(202) 797-6000

Web site: www.brookings.edu

Founded in 1927, the institution conducts research and analyzes global events and their impact on the United Sates and U.S. foreign policy. It publishes the quarterly *Brookings Review* as well as numerous books and research papers on foreign policy, many of which feature China.

CATO Institute

1000 Massachusetts Ave. NW, Washington, DC   20001-5403

(202) 842-0200

Web site: www.cato.org

The Cato Institute is a nonpartisan libertarian public policy research foundation that promotes the principles of limited government, individual liberty, and peace. Relations with China are a major research area within the institute's division of foreign policy studies. The institute regularly publishes policy analysis reports and op-eds that focus on foreign policy and trade issues involving China.

Center for Security Policy (CSP)

1901 Pennsylvania Ave. NW, Suite 201

Washington, DC   20006

(202) 835-9077

Web site: www.security-policy.org

The Center for Security Policy's mission is to stimulate debate about all aspects of security policy, notably those policies regarding the foreign, defense, economic, financial, and technology interests of the United States. It believes that China poses a threat to U.S. national security, and warns of this in many of its press releases and position statements.

Center for Strategic and International Studies (CSIS)

1800 K St. NW, Suite 400, Washington, DC   20006
(202) 887-0200 • fax: (202) 775-3199
Web site: www.csis.org

The center works to provide world leaders with strategic insights and policy options on current and emerging global issues. It publishes the *Washington Quarterly*, a journal on political, economic, and security issues, and other publications that frequently focus on China. Reports can be downloaded from its Web site.

Council on Foreign Relations

58 E. Sixty-eighth St., New York, NY   10021
(212) 434-9400 • fax: (212) 434-9800
e-mail: communications@cfr.org
Web site: www.cfr.org

The council researches the international aspects of American economic and political policies. Its journal *Foreign Affairs*, published five times a year, provides analysis on global situations, including those pertaining to China.

Embassy of the People's Republic of China in the United States of America

2300 Connecticut Ave. NW, Washington, DC   20008
(202) 328-2500
Web site: www.china-embassy.org

The embassy's news updates and white papers detail the official Chinese government positions on such issues as Taiwan, China's entry into the World Trade Organization, and human rights. Its publications include the white papers "The One-China Principle and the Taiwan Issue" and "The Progress of Human Rights in China," which can be found on its Web site.

Freedom House

1301 Connecticut Ave. NW, Floor 6, Washington, DC   20036
(202) 296-5101 • fax: (202) 293-2840
e-mail: info@freedomhouse.org
Web site: www.freedomhouse.org

Freedom House promotes human rights, democracy, free market economics, the rule of law, and independent media around the world. It publishes *Freedom in the World*, an annual comparative assessment of the state of political rights and civil liberties in 191 countries. China is consistently ranked by Freedom House as Not Free, and Freedom House publishes other reports and articles about the status of human rights in that country.

The Heritage Foundation

214 Massachusetts Ave. NE, Washington, DC   20002-4999
(202) 546-4400 • fax: (202) 546-8328
e-mail: info@heritage.org
Web site: www.heritage.org

The Heritage Foundation is a conservative think tank that formulates and promotes public policies based on the principles of free enterprise, limited government, individual freedom, traditional American values, and a strong national defense. It publishes many position papers on U.S.-China policy, such as "US-China Trade: Do's and Don'ts for Congress" and "North Korea's Nuclear Defiance."

Hoover Institution

434 Galvez Mall, Stanford, CA   94305-6010
(650) 723-1754 • fax: (650) 723-1687
e-mail: lmaune@stanford.edu
Web site: www.hoover.org

The Hoover Institution is a public policy research center housed at Stanford Univeristy devoted to advanced study of politics, economics, and political economy—both domestic and foreign—as well as international affairs. It publishes the quarterly *Hoover Digest*, which often includes articles on China, as well as a newsletter.

Human Rights in China (HRIC)
350 Fifth Ave., Suite 3311, New York, NY 10118
(212) 239-4495 • fax: (212) 239-2561
e-mail: hrichina@hrichina.org
Web site: www.hrichina.org

HRIC is an international nongovernmental organization founded by Chinese scientists and scholars. It monitors the implementation of international human rights standards in the People's Republic of China and carries out human rights advocacy and education among Chinese people inside and outside the country. HRIC's publications include the *China Rights Forum* as well as books, recordings, and reports on the status of human rights in China.

Human Rights Watch
350 Fifth Ave., 34th Floor, New York, NY 10118-3299
(212) 290-4700
e-mail: hrwnyc@hrw.org
Web site: www.hrw.org

Human Rights Watch is an international advocacy organization whose goal is to raise awareness about human rights and to investigate and expose human rights violations. It publishes annual reports about human rights around the world as well as special reports on China's treatment of its citizens and the people of Taiwan.

Institute for Policy Studies
1112 Sixteenth St. NW, Suite 600, Washington, DC 20036
(202) 234-9382
e-mail: info@ips-dc.org
Web site: www.ips-dc.org

The goal of the Institute for Policy Studies is to empower people to build healthy and democratic societies in communities, the United States, and around the world. It is the publisher of the Web page Foreign Policy in Focus (www.fpif.org), which offers briefings and reports on major developments in U.S. foreign policy regarding China.

National Endowment for Democracy (NED)
1101 Fifteenth St. NW, Suite 700, Washington, DC   20005
(202) 293-9072 • fax: (202) 223-6042
e-mail: info@ned.org
Web site: www.ned.org

The National Endowment for Democracy (NED) is a private, nonprofit organization created in 1983 to strengthen democratic institutions around the world through nongovernmental efforts. It publishes the bimonthly periodical *Journal of Democracy*.

Bibliography of Books

Ted Galen
Carpenter
America's Coming War with China: A Collision Course over Taiwan. New York: Palgrave Macmillan, 2005.

Frank Ching
China: The Truth About Its Human Rights Record. London: Ebury, 2008.

Mike Chinoy
Meltdown: The Inside Story of the North Korean Nuclear Crisis. New York: St. Martin's, 2008.

Deirdre Chethem
Before the Deluge: The Vanishing World of the Yangtze's Three Gorges. New York: Palgrave Macmillan, 2002.

Bernard D. Cole
The Great Wall at Sea: China's Navy Enters the Twenty-first Century. Annapolis, MD: U.S. Naval Institute Press, 2001.

Elizabeth C.
Economy
The River Runs Black: The Environmental Challenge to China's Future. Ithaca, NY: Cornell University Press, 2004.

James Fallows
Postcards from Tomorrow Square: Reports from China. New York: Random House, 2009.

Rob Gifford
China Road: A Journey into the Future of a Rising Power. New York: Random House, 2007.

Alexandra Harney
The China Price: The True Cost of Chinese Competitive Advantage. London: Penguin, 2008.

Mun S. Ho and Chris P. Nielson, eds. *Clearing the Air: The Health and Economic Damages of Air Pollution in China.* Cambridge, MA: MIT Press, 2007.

Yasheng Huang *Capitalism with Chinese Characteristics: Entrepreneurship and the State.* New York: Cambridge University Press.

Will Hutton *The Writing on the Wall: Why We Must Embrace China as a Partner or Face It as an Enemy.* New York: Free Press, 2006.

Blaine Kaltman *Under the Heel of the Dragon: Islam, Racism, Crime, and the Uighur in China.* Athens: Ohio University Press, 2007.

James Kynge *China Shakes the World: A Titan's Rise and Troubled Future—and the Challenge for America.* New York: Houghton Mifflin, 2006.

David M. Lampton *The Three Faces of Chinese Power: Might, Money, and Minds.* Berkeley and Los Angeles: University of California Press, 2008.

James Mann *The China Fantasy: How Our Leaders Explain Away Chinese Repression.* New York: Penguin, 2007.

David Matas and David Kilgour *Bloody Harvest: Organ Harvesting of Falun Gong Practitioners in China.* Woodstock, Ontario: Seraphim, 2009.

Andrew C. Mertha	*The Politics of Piracy: Intellectual Property in Contemporary China.* Ithaca, NY: Cornell University Press, 2007.
Paul Midler	*Poorly Made in China: An Insider's Account of the Tactics Behind China's Production Game.* Hoboken, NJ: Wiley, 2009.
Barry Naughton	*The Chinese Economy: Transitions and Growth.* Cambridge, MA: MIT Press, 2007.
Peter Navarro	*The Coming China Wars: Where They Will Be Fought and How They Can Be Won. Rev. and Expanded Ed..* Upper Saddle River, NJ: Pearson Education, 2008.
David Ownby	*Falun Gong and the Future of China.* New York: Oxford University Press, 2008.
Philip P. Pan	*Out of Mao's Shadow: The Struggle for the Soul of a New China.* New York: Simon & Schuster, 2008.
Dai Qing	*The River Dragon Has Come! The Three Gorges Dam and the Fate of China's Yangtze River and Its People.* Armonk, NY: M.E. Sharpe, 1998.
David Shambaugh	*China's Communist Party: Atrophy and Adaptation.* Berkeley and Los Angeles: University of California Press, 2008.

Susan L. Shirk	*China: Fragile Superpower: How China's Internal Politics Could Derail Its Peaceful Rise.* New York: Oxford University Press, 2007.
Warren W. Smith Jr.	*China's Tibet: Autonomy or Assimilation.* Lanham, MD: Rowman & Littlefield, 2008.
Ligang Song and Wing Thye Woo, eds.	*China's Dilemma: Economic Growth, the Environment, and Climate Change.* Washington, DC: Brookings Institution Press, 2008.
Nancy Bernkopf Tucker	*Strait Talk: United States-Taiwan Relations and the Crisis with China.* Cambridge, MA: Harvard University Press, 2009.
Graham Turner	*The Credit Crunch: Housing Bubbles, Globalisation and the Worldwide Economic Crisis.* Ann Arbor, MI: Pluto Press, 2008.
Minky Worden	*China's Great Leap: The Beijing Games and Olympian Human Rights Challenges.* New York: Seven Stories, 2008.

Index

A

Ablikim Abdiriyim, 61–62
Acemoglu, Daron, 35
Acid rain pollution, 173
Adams, Brad, 60
Administrations for Industry &
   Commerce (AIC), 101
Advanced anti-ship cruise missiles
   (ASCMs), 133
AFL-CIO Industrial Union Coun-
   cil, 89, 92–93
Africa, 121, 176
Aircraft parts, counterfeiting, 109
Air pollution
   cars and, 166, 168, 173
   coal and, 171–172, 173, 189
   cooperative collaboration
      against, 178–179
   economy and, 165–166
   export impact from, 176–178
   gross domestic product and,
      172, 173, 175–176
   health effect from, 174–175
   long-term improvement, 168–
      169
   reforms for, 166–168
   regional impact of, 171
American military hegemony, 130
Amnesty International, 20, 54–62
Anti-China propaganda, 73–75
Anti-ship ballistic missiles, 133
Applebaum, Anne, 140–143
Asia Times (newspaper), 17
Authoritarianism, 19, 22–23, 25–
   27, 28–30

B

Bandow, Doug, 129–134
Bank lending concerns, 81
Barro, Robert J., 34, 35
Baugh, Robert, 89, 91
Beech, Hannah, 162
Beijing government
   as authoritarian, 19, 22–23,
      28–29
   clean energy needs, 187, 190
   climate change and, 189
   criminal justice system and,
      56
   economic development and,
      147
   human rights and, 22–23, 52
   Internet piracy and, 113–114
   legal reform in, 24–25, 53
   nationalism and, 27, 37
   pollution and, 165–169, 176,
      177
   property rights and, 87
   reforms, 26–27
   religion and, 60
   SARS outbreak in, 162, 163
   security concerns and, 146,
      148
   soft rights law and, 45
   Taiwan relations with, 128,
      150, 156–158
   Tiananmen Square massacre,
      16, 17
   trade imbalances and, 95
   unemployment and, 25–26
   yifazhiguo and, 49
   See also Military capability;
      Olympic Games (2008)

Bezlova, Antoaneta, 17
Black carbon (BC) soot, 172, 174
Blodget, Henry, 112–117
Bootleg DVDs, 108–109, 113–114
Bo Xilai, 85
Buddhists, 42, 58
Burma, 128
Bush, George W. (administration)
    air pollution and, 178
    democracy in China and, 22,
        23, 28
    North Korea and, 136
    nuclear weapons and, 138
    security strategy of, 124
    trade deficit and, 91–93

C

Campbell, Kurt, 124
Carbon dioxide (CO_2) levels, 173–
    174, 178, 186, 187
Carbon monoxide levels, 166
Caterpillar Inc., 86
Cato Institute, 85
Central Asia, 128
Chak Chan, 166
Chamber of Commerce (U.S.),
    99–106
Chan, John, 16
Chang, Leslie T., 14, 42
Chen Chu, 151
Chen Guangcheng, 56
Chen Shui-bian, 152, 157, 158
Chiang Kai-shek, 155, 158
China Meteorological Administra-
    tion, 173
*China's Communist Party Atrophy
    and Adaptation* (Shambaugh), 41
The Chinese Century (Shenkar),
    114

Chinese Communist Party (CCP)
    criminal justice system and,
        56
    democracy in China and, 23–
        24, 40, 43
    ideological shift of, 37
    policy on Taiwan, 150
    religion and, 19
    U.S. trade deficit and, 60–61
Chinese Pottermania, 103
Chinese Supreme Court, 51
Chin-Hao Hung, 120
Chou, Jennifer, 26
Christians/Christianity, 57, 58–59
Chu Shulong, 125
Civil liberties, 32, 36
Clark, Helen, 163
Clean Air Act, 178
Climate change
    addressing, 182–183
    carbon dioxide (CO_2) levels,
        173–174, 178, 186, 187
    current trends, 183–184
    greenhouse gas (GHG) emis-
        sions, 172–173, 187, 188
    pollution and, 181–182
Clinton, Bill (administration), 22,
    23, 64, 124
Clinton, Hillary, 64–67, 95, 186
Coal pollution, 171–172, 173, 189
Cole, J. Michael, 149–153
Committee Against Torture
    (CAT), 57
Communism
    capitalism and, 27
    dominance of, 30, 49, 66
    in Eastern Europe, 15
    economy and, 37, 70
    human rights and, 49, 52
    open society concept of, 43
    religion and, 19

secrecy and, 162
support for, 15, 16
transfer of power and, 41–42
Computer manufacturing, 102
Confucius (Chinese philosopher), 37
Constitution, versions of, 48
Convention on the Elimination of All Forms of Discrimination Against Women, 48
Coonan, Clifford, 154–159, 163
Counterfeiting rings, 104
Counterfeit product seizures, 100
Criminal justice system, 56
Crop yields, 172
Cuba, 128
Cultural Revolution, 52
Currency devalued, 95–96
Czechoslovakia, 15

D

Dalai Lama, 60
Death sentence statistics, 57–58
Defense Department (U.S.), 127, 131–134
Defense policies
  budget for, 126, 130, 133
  control of, 70, 148
  economy and, 76
  global spending, 132
Demining in Taiwan, 155–157
Democracy
  anti-Americanism and, 27–28
  authoritarianism *vs.*, 25–27, 28–30
  Bush, George W. and, 22, 23, 28
  communism and, 23–24, 40, 43
  daily life and, 25–27

economic liberty and, 33–34
electoral, 35–36
inevitability of, 23–25, 36–38, 40–41
middle class and, 42, 43
non-democracy *vs.*, 53
U.S. interests and, 22–23, 29
Democratic Progressive Party (DPP), 150–151, 152–153, 157
Deng Xiaoping, 15–16, 52
Denuclearization. *See* Nuclear nonproliferation
Detention centers, 56–57
Dongfeng 31 (DF-31A) missile, 124
Dorgan, Byron, 84
Dorn, James A., 83–87
Drug rings, 104
Dust pollution, 173
DVDs, bootlegged, 108–109, 113–114

E

Earthquake damage, 163
Eastern Europe, 15
East Germany, 141, 142
Economic and Social Council (UN), 47
Economic Policy Institute (EPI), 89, 91
Economy
  air pollution and, 165–166
  bank lending and, 81
  devalued currency and, 95–96
  global changes, 81–82
  global recession impact on, 72–76, 77–82
  growth of, 33–34
  Hong Kong and, 70–71
  job availability, 86

modernization of, 25
rebalancing, 75–76
slow recovery of, 78–81
Western economy *vs.*, 74
See also Gross Domestic Product
Education
    anti-piracy action and, 115
    demagogue resistance and, 33
    democracy and, 34
    improvements in, 32, 36, 41
    labor camps and, 51, 55–57, 59
    "Patriotic Education" campaign, 60
    religious, 61
    rule-of-law cooperation, 24, 29
Education, Science and Culture Organization (UN), 47
Einstein, Albert, 139
Elections/electoral democracy, 35–36, 38
Elimination of All Forms of Discrimination Against Women, 48
Energy efficiency improvements, 75
Environmental Program (UN), 166
Epoch Times (newspaper), 20
Eritrea, 121
Ethiopia, 121
Export concerns, 17, 79, 96

F

Falun Gong, 19–20, 56, 57, 59
Far Eastern Economic Review (FEER), 114, 116
Financial Times (newspaper), 75–76

Fixed-peg system, 97–98
Forbes (magazine), 15
Freedom House (FH), 32, 34, 36
Freedom of expression, 55, 58–59
Freedom rating, 32, 34
Free trade
    actions needed for, 89–91
    debt issues and, 91–93
    forced trading, 85–87
    logic behind, 84–85
    U.S. trade deficit and, 89

G

Gao Zhisheng, 50
Gates, Bill, 91, 120
G-3 economies, 79
Geithner, Timothy, 95
Geneva Convention, 47
Germany, 14, 188
Global energy crisis, 66
Global recession, 72–76, 77–82
Global Times (newspaper), 28
Government. *See* Beijing government
Graham, Lindsey, 87, 92
Greenhouse gas (GHG) emissions
    climate change and, 183
    international concern over, 178, 187–188
    rates of, 172–173
Green technologies, 190
Griswold, Daniel, 85, 86
Gross Domestic Product (GDP)
    air pollution and, 172, 173, 175–176
    climate change and, 183
    energy consumption and, 75, 76
    fiscal deficit and, 81
    growth rate of, 14, 80

per capita (GDPpc), 32–34
piracy/counterfeiting and, 114
trade deficit and, 91
Groundwater depletion, 181–182
Guangdong pollution, 167, 168–169
Guardian (newspaper), 14

H

"Harmonious Society" program, 26, 41
Harper, Stephen, 73
Harry Potter sequels, 103
Havel, Vaclav, 64
Hayward, Steven, 180–184
Health care improvements, 41
Health effect from pollution, 174–175
Heart (journal), 174
Hegemony and military capability, 127–128
High Commissioner for Human Rights (OHCHR), 45, 46–47
Hong Kong, 70–71, 87, 158, 175, 176
Hope, Bruce, 177
Hsiao Bi-khim, 150–151, 152
Hu Jintao, 26, 41, 92
Hu Yaobang, 15–16
Huang Qi, 57
Hui Zhang, 144–148
Human rights
abuses, 27, 54–62, 64–67
action plan for, 49
authoritarian government and, 22–23
civil liberties and, 32, 36
Falun Gong and, 19–20, 56, 59

improvements, 51–53
justice system and, 55–58
legal formalism and, 46
Tibet and, 59–62
U.S. interest in, 66–67
Human rights laws
adopting, 45–46
advantages to, 50–51
limitations of, 48–50
treaties for, 46–48
Hume, David, 84–85, 87
Hungary, 15

I

India, 138, 139, 176, 188
Intellectual property rights (IPR) issues
Action Plans for, 101–102
avoiding piracy, 112–117, 190
bootleg DVDs, 108–109, 113–114
business leadership and, 109–111
commitment needed for, 102–105, 115–117
enforcement of, 105–106
solutions for, 108–109
violations of, 100
Intercontinental Ballistic Missiles (ICBMs), 124
International Atomic Energy Agency (IAEA), 137
International Covenant on Civil and Political Rights, 48
International Covenant on Economic, Social and Cultural Rights, 48
International Labor Organization (ILO), 47

International Monetary Fund (IMF), 78, 79
Internet, 24, 25, 55, 58, 105, 113
Iran, 123, 128, 137, 138

J

Japan
    acid rain pollution and, 173
    China threat to, 125–127, 143
    democracy and, 35–36
    GDP and, 76
    greenhouse gas emissions and, 188
    human rights treaties with, 45
    North Korea relations and, 146, 147
    Taiwanese independence and, 150
    U.S. trade deficit and, 92
Jiang Zemin, 41
"JIN" (type 094) class nuclear submarine, 124
Jobs
    availability, 42, 86, 96
    education and, 36
    lawyers and, 55–56
    unemployment, 25–26, 81
    U.S. and, 84–85, 86, 89–92, 95
Journal of Toxicology and Environmental Health (journal), 175

K

Kalathil, Shanthi, 162
Kim, Juli S., 170–179
Kim Jong Il, 143
KMT party (Taiwan), 153, 157, 158
Knockoff pharmaceuticals, 108–109

Korea, 76, 92, 137, 145, 148, 173
Korean War armistice, 141, 147
Kroeber, Arthur, 39–43
Kyoto Protocol, 172

L

Labour camps, 51, 56–57, 59
Laws/lawmaking
    justice system and, 55–58
    legal profession and, 50–51, 55–56
    problems with, 49–50
    reforms for, 52–53
    See also Human rights laws
Legal formalism, 46
Lenin, Vladimir (Leninists), 37
Lestz, Michael, 19
Lhasa (Tibet) protests, 55
Li Heng, 167
Li Hongzhi, 19
Li Xiannian, 128
Lieberthal, Kenneth, 189
Lipset, Martin, 15–17, 33
Liu Xiaobo, 58
Liu Yazhou, 128
Lu Xiao-rong, 157

M

Ma Ying-jeou, 150, 152, 153, 156, 157
Malin, Martin, 144–148
Manufacturing industries, 96
Mao Zedong, 15, 16, 155, 169
Marxist-Leninist theory, 37
Massachusetts Institute of Technology (MIT), 189–190
McCain, John, 136
Mercury pollution, 176–177

Merrill Lynch (Asia Pacific division), 176
Microsoft, 115, 117
Military capability
    buildup concerns, 123–125, 131, 133
    defense budget and, 126
    as global threat, 125–127
    hegemony and, 127–128
    increases in, 120, 124
    naval procurement program, 124
    not a threat, 129–134
    nuclear nonproliferation, 136–139
    as U.S. threat, 122–128, 133–134
    See also Defense policies
Ming wan, 44–53
Ministry of Public Security, 25–26
Multimedia Innovation Centre, 70
Muslims, 58
Muslim Uighurs, 60, 61–62

N

Nathan, Andrew, 41
National Geographic (magazine), 14
The National Interest (magazine), 32
Nationalism, 27–28
National People's Congress (NPC), 45, 47, 50
National People's Congress Standing Committee (NPCSC), 45, 47
Naval procurement program, 124
Navarro, Peter, 94–98
The New England Journal of Medicine (journal), 174
New Zealand, 163

Nielson, Jeff, 72–76
Non-democracy, 53
Nongovernmental organizations (NGOs), 26, 178
North Atlantic Treaty Organization (NATO), 121
"North Face" jackets, 114–115
North Korea
    acid rain pollution and, 173
    backing from China, 140–143
    breaks armistice, 147
    confrontation by China, 144–148
    democracy and, 35
    nuclear ambitions of, 127–128, 145
    nuclear nonproliferation and, 136–137, 138–139
    oil exports to, 141
    Six Party talks, 145–146
    treaties and, 48
Not Free category, 32, 34, 35
Nuclear capability, 123, 124–128, 130–131
Nuclear nonproliferation, 136–139
Nuclear Nonproliferation Treaty (NPT), 138
Nuclear Suppliers Group (NSG), 137

O

Obama, Barack (administration)
    China and, 142–143
    global financial market and, 98
    green technologies and, 190
    human rights and, 66–67
    nuclear security agenda of, 136, 147
    pollution concerns and, 187

Office of the United Nations High Commissioner for Human Rights (OHCHR), 45, 46–47
Oil exports, 141
Olympic Games (2008)
    air pollution and, 165–168, 177
    human rights issues and, 55, 56
    "protest zones" over, 58
    religious freedom and, 20, 58–59
Open society concept, 43

P

Paltsal Kyab, 61
Parks, James, 88–93
Partly Free category, 32, 34, 35
"Patriotic Education" campaign, 60
Paulson, Henry, 87
Peacekeeping involvement, 120–121
Peer-to-peer Web sites (P-2-P), 105
The Pentagon
    Chinese defense budget and, 130
    Chinese military buildup concerns, 123–125, 131, 133
    "hedging" strategy with China, 128
Pentagon's Quadrennial Defense Review (QDR), 123–124, 128
People's Daily (newspaper), 139
People's Liberation Army's (PLA), 16, 124, 125, 127, 130
People's Republic of China (PRC), 48, 102, 104
Persson, Torsten, 35

Pham, Peter, 121
Pharmaceutical knockoffs, 108–109
Piracy of goods. *See* Intellectual property rights
Pluralism, 27
Poland, 15
Politics/political freedom, 14–15, 28–30, 51
    See also Beijing government; Democracy
Pollution
    addressing, 182–183
    in Beijing, 165–169, 176, 177
    black carbon (BC) soot, 172, 174
    climate change and, 181–182
    global security and, 66
    health effects, 174–175
    with manufacturing, 96
    mercury and, 176–177
    sulfur dioxide (SO$_2$), 166, 172, 173, 175, 182
    types of, 173
    United States and, 177, 178–179
Pre-loaded legal software, 102
Prezworski, Adam, 35
"Protest zones," 58
Purchasing Managers' Index (PMI), 78

Q

Qin Dahe, 173
Quiet submarines, 133

R

Radio Free Asia, 26

Radio Free Europe/Radio Liberty Online, 16
Rahn, Kenneth, 167
Rebiya Kadeer, 61
Recknagal, Charles, 16
Rein, Shaun, 108–110
Religion
    Buddhists, 42, 58
    communism and, 19
    education and, 61
    Falun Gong and, 19–20, 56, 57, 59
    freedom of, 19, 20, 58–59
    Muslims, 58
    Muslim Uighurs, 60, 61–62
    Olympic Games (2008) and, 20, 58, 59
    persecution and, 57, 60–62, 61
Religion in the News (magazine), 19
Renewable energy sources, 187–188
"Resilient Authoritarianism," 41
Retail sales indicators, 79, 81
Rossett, Claudia, 15
Roubini, Nouriel, 77–82
Rowen, Henry S., 31–38
Rule-of-law cooperation, 24, 29
Russia, 27

S

Sandalow, David, 189
Savings rates, 81–82
Schumer, Charles, 87, 92
Scott, Robert, 91, 92
Seager, Ashley, 14
Security Council (UN), 142, 145, 146
Seligsohn, Deborah, 168–169

Severe acute respiratory syndrome (SARS), 162–163
Shambaugh, David, 41
Shen Dingli, 125
Shenkar, Oded, 114, 116
Short-range ballistic missiles (SRBM), 127
Singapore, 35, 176
Sinitic societies, 35, 36
Six Party talks, 145–146, 148
Slavery Convention, 47
Social welfare, 25
Soft rights law, 45
Software pirating, 104–105
Solar Electric Power Association (SEPA), 173, 182, 183
Saudi Arabia, 48
South Korea
    acid rain pollution and, 173
    democracy and, 35–36
    North Korea relations, 143, 146, 147
Soviet Union, 15, 41, 167
Stokes, Bruce, 185–190
Stratfor, 120
Sudan, 120, 128
Sulfur dioxide (SO_2) pollution, 166, 172, 173, 175, 182
Supreme People's Court, 103
Swine flu, 163

T

Tabellini, Guido, 35
Taiwan
    China's threat to, 123, 125–127, 131, 133, 143, 149–153
    demining of beaches, 155–157
    democracy and, 35–36

improved relations with
China, 154–159
independence and, 150–151
North Korea relations and,
147
pandas for peace, 158–159
Taiwan Relations Act, 127
Taiyanggong, China, 186, 190
Terrorism concerns
at Olympic Games (2008), 55
Uighur Muslims and, 60, 61,
148
U.S. prosecution of, 128, 146
Terrorism-sponsor list (U.S.), 136
Tiananmen Square massacre, 15–
17, 33, 53
Tibet, 55, 59–62
Tibetan organizations, 59
Tkacik, John J., Jr., 122–128
Torture prevalence, 55
Trade imbalances, 95–98
Tran, Tini, 164–169
Treaties for human rights, 46–48
Troedsson, Hans, 163
Tuan Tuan (panda), 155, 158–159

U

Uighur Muslims, 60–62, 148
Unemployment concerns, 25–26,
81
United Nations (UN)
China and, 52
Environmental Program, 166
General Assembly, 47, 58
human rights issues, 45
joint missions by, 120
nuclear nonproliferation and,
136–137
religious freedom and, 19

Security Council, 142, 145,
146
United States (U.S.)
Chamber of Commerce, 99–
106
Chinese mistrust of, 28
debt issues in, 91–93
Defense Department, 127,
131–134
democracy and, 22–23, 29
economic crisis in, 66
free trade with China, 83–87,
88–93
interest in human rights,
66–67
job statistics for, 90
North Korean threat and,
144–148
pollution from China and,
177, 178–179
rule-of-law cooperation, 24,
29
security strategy of, 128
Six Party talks, 145–146, 148
terrorism-sponsor list, 136
See also Obama, Barack; The
Pentagon
U.S.-China Economic and Security
Review Commission, 89
U.S.-China Joint Commission on
Trade (JCCT), 102, 104, 105

V

Venezuela, 128
Vietnam, 35
Voice of America, 29

W

Wall Street Journal (newspaper),
73–75, 76
Wang Lequan, 61

Wang Qian-yong, 158
Wang Xiaoming, 169
Wang Zhen, 16
War on Terrorism, 128
Wei Jingsheng, 63–67
Wen Jiabao, 41
Western economy, 74
Williamette River, Oregon pollution, 177
Wolf, David, 107–111
World Health Organization (WHO), 157, 163, 173, 177, 181
World Socialist Web, 16
World Trade Organization (WTO), 86, 87, 91, 172
Wu Bangguo, 47
Wu Shumin, 150, 152
Wu Tseng-dong, 155–156
Wu Yi, 87, 102

X

Xiaohui Anne Wu, 135–139
Xi Jinping, 41

Xinjiang Uighur Autonomous Region (XUAR), 55, 60–62
Xinmin Evening News (newspaper), 42
Xu Demin, 165, 169
Xu Na, 59

Y

Yamaha motorcycles, 114
Yeh Ching-chuan, 150, 159
Yifazhiguo (governing according to law), 49
Ying Ma, 21–30
Yu, Frank, 70
Yuan value, 96–98
Yuan Weijing, 56
Yuan Yuan (panda), 155, 158–159
Yu Zhou, 59

Z

Zhao Ziyang, 16
Zhu Chenghu, 125
Zimbabwe, 128